MW01167345

THE FIGHT FOR THE FUTURE

*How People Defeated Hollywood and Saved
the Internet—For Now*

Edward Lee

"This is the story about the people behind the most important first battle for the future. When that revolution is won, we will look back to the fight against SOPA/PIPA the way Americans look back to the first shots at Lexington. Beautifully written, and powerfully compelling, this is a must read for anyone who wants a glimpse of where we are going."

—Lawrence Lessig, Roy L. Furman Professor of Law and Leadership, Harvard Law School

"Edward Lee's absorbing account is more than a story about the fight against unwise legislation; it is also a remarkable tale about new forms of political organization and how they can help keep the Internet free for everyone to use and enjoy."

—Jack M. Balkin, Director, the Information Society Project at Yale Law School

"Professor Lee's book reveals the true story of the fight to stop SOPA, and the historic effort to protect the Internet and Internet freedoms in 2012. Since that time there has been plenty of speculation—much of it wrong—about what happened. It's wonderful to see such a full and complete recounting of the historic events, told in an engaging manner that is hard to put down."

—Mike Masnick, Founder and Editor, Techdirt

About the Author

Edward Lee is a professor of law and the Director of the internationally recognized Program in Intellectual Property Law at IIT Chicago-Kent College of Law. He graduated summa cum laude from Williams College with a bachelor's degree in philosophy and classics, and cum laude from Harvard Law School.

He has written extensively about copyright, the Internet, free speech, and the history of the freedom of the press. His article *Freedom of the Press 2.0* was selected as one of the best First Amendment articles of 2008 and as one of the year's best articles related to intellectual property for 2008-2009. He is a co-author of a leading casebook on International Intellectual Property published by West. Previously, he worked at the Stanford Center for Internet and Society, including on *Eldred v. Ashcroft* and *Golan v. Holder*, two of the most significant cases involving the First Amendment and copyright law. As a contributor to the *Huffington Post*, he has written various articles related to the Internet, copyright, and pop culture. His *Boston Review* article "The Day Wikipedia Went Dark" was published on the one-year anniversary of the Wikipedia blackout. He can be contacted via Twitter @edleeprof.

To my parents

Contents

Preface iii

Timeline of Key Events v

Introduction 1

1. Free Bieber 7
2. American Censorship Day 35
3. Bring in the Nerds 55
4. Wikipedia Blackout 79
5. NO to ACTA 105
6. Hello, Democracy 129

Acknowledgments 149

Notes 153

Preface

Writing about events involving thousands of people is terribly unsatisfying. Inevitably, details about the events, including many people who helped to shape them, must be left out. There is simply not enough time—or pages—to canvas every detail and every person related to an event of such magnitude in a book that is digestible.

This book is no exception. I have done my best, however, to provide an accurate portrayal of the historic events surrounding the mass protests in 2012 against two controversial copyright proposals (SOPA and ACTA) that people feared would lead to Internet censorship. My portrayal is, by no means, meant as an exhaustive account of these events. Although I interviewed numerous people involved in the events (over 60 people in the United States and Europe), I was not able to interview many more people who had a significant role in the events, despite my (sometimes desperate) efforts to track them down. And even with the people I did interview, I sometimes had to make difficult decisions to cut out mention of their involvement from my book due to space or editing reasons. Their omission from the book is meant in no way to minimize their important contributions.

Timeline of Key Events

October 23, 2007
   -United States announces anti-piracy initiative called the Anti-Counterfeiting Trade Agreement (ACTA) with trading partners

May 12, 2011
   -Anti-piracy bills PROTECT IP Act (PIPA) and Commercial Felony Streaming Act (CFSA) introduced in U.S. Senate

May 26, 2011
   -Five leading Internet engineers issue white paper on anti-piracy bill's potential threat to cybersecurity through DNS blocking

September 2011
   -Center for Rights plans initiative called Fight for the Future to oppose PIPA and CFSA

October 1, 2011
   -United States, Australia, Canada, Korea, Japan, New Zealand, Morocco, and Singapore sign ACTA in Tokyo; the European Union and its members expected to sign in January 2012

October 19, 2011
   -Fight for the Future launches "Free Bieber" campaign against CFSA

October 26, 2011

-Anti-piracy bill Stop Online Piracy Act (SOPA) introduced in U.S. House

November 9, 2011

-Mozilla hosts a "brown bag" meeting for Internet companies, nonprofits, activists, and congressional staffers to plan protest against SOPA/PIPA

November 16, 2011

-House Judiciary Committee holds hearings on SOPA
-American Censorship Day held with websites blacking out and people calling Congress to oppose SOPA

December 15–16, 2011

-House Judiciary Committee holds markup on SOPA, but cannot finish before recess

December 22–23, 2011

-Reddit user starts protest to transfer domain names from GoDaddy due to its support of SOPA
-GoDaddy changes its support of SOPA to opposition

January 14, 2012

-Obama Administration responds to "We the People" petitions and opposes SOPA/PIPA's potential harm to free speech, open Internet, and cybersecurity

January 18, 2012

-Wikipedia, Google, Wired Magazine, Craigslist, Reddit, Tumblr, Wordpress, and thousands of other sites go black in largest Internet protest in history

January 19, 2012

-Polish government informs Dialogue Group including Internet NGOs that Poland would sign ACTA; NGOs object based on lack of public consultations

-Effects of U.S. and New Zealand governments' shutdown of Megaupload site felt in Europe

January 20, 2012
-Congress indefinitely suspends consideration of SOPA and PIPA bills due to protests

January 24–25, 2012
-Massive street protests against ACTA involving thousands of people in 50 cities in Poland

February 11, 2012
-Massive street protests against ACTA involving over 100,000 people in 250 cities in 27 EU countries

February 25, 2012
-More street protests held against ACTA in EU countries

June 9, 2012
-Final round of mass street protests held against ACTA in EU countries

June 21, 2012
-EU Parliament's International Trade committee recommends (19 to 12) rejecting ACTA

July 4, 2012
-EU Parliament rejects ACTA by a landslide vote of 478 to 39

The people are the only legitimate fountain of power, and it is from them that the constitutional charter, under which the several branches of government hold their power, is derived.

—JAMES MADISON, THE FEDERALIST NO. 49

By giving people the power to share, we are starting to see people make their voices heard on a different scale from what has historically been possible. These voices will increase in number and volume. They cannot be ignored. Over time, we expect governments will become more responsive to issues and concerns raised directly by all their people rather than through intermediaries controlled by a select few.

Through this process, we believe that leaders will emerge across all countries who are pro-internet and fight for the rights of their people, including the right to share what they want and the right to access all information that people want to share with them.

—MARK ZUCKERBERG, THE HACKER WAY

Introduction

On April 18, 1775, a silversmith living in colonial America made a midnight ride that has become the subject of legends. For decades studied by school children and revered by citizens throughout the United States, the now famous midnight ride symbolizes the courage of a lone messenger who sounded the alarm about the incoming British troops.

As Henry Wadsworth Longfellow commemorated nearly a century later in a poem that itself became famous:

> So through the night rode Paul Revere;
> And so through the night went his cry of alarm
> To every Middlesex village and farm,—
> A cry of defiance, and not of fear,
> A voice in the darkness, a knock at the door,
> And a word that shall echo for evermore![1]

There's a small problem, though, with this famous account. It's untrue.

As Pulitzer Prize winning historian David Hackett Fischer has shown in his book *Paul Revere's Ride*, the idea that Paul Revere sounded the alarm alone during the night is romanticized. And simply wrong: "[I]t is not what actually happened that night. Many other riders helped Paul Revere to carry the alarm."[2]

More important than debunking the myths surrounding the

famous midnight ride, Fischer explains the main reason why Paul Revere and the other midnight riders were able to warn the people in Massachusetts so effectively and swiftly. The riders had organized ahead of time a *decentralized network*. Through this network, many people could spread the warning to whomever and by however they saw fit—word of mouth, gunshots, bell-ringing, drums, or the proverbial lantern in the church tower.

Unlike the centralized intelligence system of the British army, the American system operated "from the bottom up," with townsfolk sounding the alarm.[3] As Fischer describes, the riders "enlisted [each town's] churches and ministers, its physicians and lawyers, its family networks and voluntary associations."[4] The key was that this American network was "coordinated through an open, disorderly network of congresses and committees, but no central authority."[5]

Revere was a key figure that night, no doubt, and rightfully revered. But he was just a small part of a decentralized network that effectively sounded the alarm about the incoming British troops. That network—of which Revere was only a part—helped secure an important first victory for early America at the Battles of Lexington and Concord. Without the network, Revere's cry of alarm would have been all for naught.

*　　*　　*

At midnight on January 18, 2012, a decentralized network figured just as prominently as a warning system to Americans as the one Revere and the other midnight riders utilized on April 18, 1775. Only this time, the network consisted of websites, not horses.

Websites ranging from the most trafficked in the world, including Google and Wikipedia, all the way down to small, personal blogs, joined in a massive blackout of their sites. Thousands of websites protested a controversial copyright bill, the Stop Online Piracy Act (SOPA), which people feared would impose a regime of censorship on the Internet. Wikipedia provided the most stunning visual of the day, an ominous blackened home page warning: "the U.S. Congress is considering legislation that could fatally damage the free and open Internet."[6]

Protecting the "free and open Internet" served as an important rallying cry that helped to galvanize millions of Americans to sign petitions, make phone calls, and organize demonstrations against SOPA. For the first time in U.S. history, people banded together to help stop a copyright bill in Congress. Copyright law was no longer an arcane area reserved for lawyers and legislators. It had now become central to many people's concerns and their everyday lives. SOPA sparked the largest online protest in history—which was perhaps best symbolized by Wikipedia blacking out all of its English-language webpages around the world for a full twenty-four hours.

Two days later, SOPA was abandoned in Congress. Many of the supporters of the bill even changed their support into outright opposition on the very day of the protest.[7]

Precisely how a copyright bill that had the full support of Hollywood and the entertainment industry, plus strong bipartisan support in Congress—the normal ingredients for easy passage—could fail so dramatically is the focus of this book.

Just as in the case of Paul Revere's ride, it's easy to romanticize one person or entity as the "hero" in stopping SOPA. Tech giant Google, which spent much time and money lobbying against SOPA, is an obvious choice of some commentators, including some of the supporters of the bill who would like to place their blame with big, bad Google. The Internet tech sector is another candidate. The "battle between Hollywood and Silicon Valley" was an attractive headline to the media—and, well, to Hollywood.[8] Another choice is Wikipedia, the free online encyclopedia run by thousands of volunteer writers around the world. Others would say Internet activists and nonprofits like Electronic Frontier Foundation, Demand Progress, and Fight for the Future. And then there's the public at large, many of whom eventually got involved in the debate by signing petitions, calling or emailing their Congress members, or voicing their opposition to SOPA on Twitter and in other ways.

So who was really responsible for stopping SOPA?

To ask that question is to misunderstand the events. To single out Google, Wikipedia, or one entity or person would be to make the same mistake as singling out Paul Revere. A diverse coalition of entities, communities, and individuals took part in the historic Internet protest on January 18, 2012 and the opposition leading up to that date. Everyone who participated in the opposition deserves credit for stopping SOPA.

And much of the credit must go to "ordinary" Americans who got involved in the public debate, who were concerned enough about SOPA to express their views to Congress in petitions, protests, tweets, emails, and phone calls. In the end, what grabbed Congress's attention the most wasn't the massive amount (tens of millions) of lobbying dollars spent on either side by Hollywood or the tech industry—that's just business as usual in Congress.[9] Instead, it was people's phone calls, emails, and other voices of opposition that changed the terms of the SOPA debate.

As Aaron Swartz, the precocious Internet activist and programmer who was one of the first to sound the alarm about SOPA, said in one of his last public speeches before his untimely death, "We won this fight because everyone made themselves the hero of their own story. Everyone took it as their job to save this crucial freedom. They threw themselves into it. They did whatever they could think of to do. They didn't stop to ask anyone for permission. . . . The Senators were right. The Internet *really* is out of control."[10]

The SOPA protests even helped to spark mass protests in Europe to oppose the Anti-Counterfeiting Trade Agreement (ACTA), another anti-piracy proposal that people in the European Union (EU) feared would lead to Internet censorship. There, people's involvement in stopping ACTA was even more obvious: tens of thousands of people demonstrated in the streets of hundreds of cities across Europe in below-freezing temperatures. Never before had people in all 27 countries of the EU demonstrated in unison to voice their collective view. The mass demonstrations led to the EU Parliament's rejection of ACTA by a landslide vote of 478 members against and only 39 in favor.

This book chronicles the way in which many different people, communities, and entities sounded the alarm about SOPA and

ACTA through a decentralized network. The Internet provided people with a way to fight for their Internet freedoms by using the networking tools that comprise the Internet, such as Facebook, Twitter, and YouTube.

Although the fight to stop SOPA and ACTA succeeded, the fight for the Internet—its future—wages on. Whether the Internet remains "free and open" is still up for grabs. Governments and corporations continue to consider new ways to regulate and police the Internet, sometimes in ways that could lead to censorship. As of yet, no constitution in any country expressly recognizes the freedom of the Internet, although some countries have begun to consider proposals for an Internet bill of rights.

The protests of 2012, however, do provide hope. They show that people can sound the alarm about threats to the freedoms they hold dear. Like Paul Revere and the other midnight riders, people today can join in "a common effort in the cause of freedom."[11] Luckily, the Internet is faster, and more effective, than a horse. But whether these efforts succeed in saving the Internet from censorship and control ultimately depends on the future we all now fight for.

Chapter 1

Free Bieber

Justin Bieber was an unlikely spokesperson to lead the opposition to a controversial copyright bill pending before Congress in 2011. The teenage pop singer was more the poster child for social media than a leader of a political cause.

Bieber owed his meteoric success to social media: he developed an enormous following of fans around the world by singing pop cover songs on YouTube starting in January 2007 at the precocious age of 12. Back then, Bieber looked tiny for his age and still had a high-pitched voice. But one thing was for sure: Bieber could sing, and sing just about anyone—Sarah McLachlin, Justin Timberlake, Chris Brown, Usher, Lil' Bow Wow, Ne-Yo, Alicia Keys, Aretha Franklin, you name it.

In each cover performance, Bieber made the song his own. And then, with the power of YouTube, he shared his performances with the world. Under the username "kidrauhl," Bieber's first music videos were from a local Idol-type singing competition—which he lost. But Bieber kept on singing and making videos of various cover songs, and his mom posted the homemade videos on YouTube.

Soon, legions of fans flocked to Bieber's music videos on YouTube and essentially discovered Bieber before any music label did. Such was the beauty of YouTube. It allowed people, as the company motto invited, to "broadcast yourself" to audiences in the millions. Within a few years of posting videos on YouTube, Bieber landed agent Scooter Braun, signed a record deal with Usher's label, sold two Platinum albums, and, perhaps most impressive of all, had the most-viewed video on YouTube at the time with a half-billion views. He also had the second most number of followers on Twitter, 27 million by 2012, over 7 million more than President Barack Obama. Fittingly, in 2012, *Billboard* awarded Bieber its first-ever Social Artist of the Year award. Bieber beat out the likes of Lady Gaga, Rihanna, Shakira, and Eminem. Not too shabby for a teenager.

Bieber's talent, of course, was singing, not political activism. In 2011, he was still too young to vote and wasn't even a U.S. citizen—he was Canadian. But, by a stroke of luck and the power of social media, Bieber would become the figurehead of the "Free Bieber" campaign—the opening salvo against SOPA and PIPA, two copyright bills in the U.S. Congress that some feared would break the Internet.

Free Bieber represented a new kind of twenty-first century political protest, one carried out online through social media, blogs, Facebook pages, YouTube videos, tweets, and online petitions. The movement spread quickly, in real time, mobilizing people at the grassroots level through social media and utilizing the very speech tools of the Internet that the movement sought to protect. And the movement had a wry, almost cheeky sense of humor fitting for the free Internet culture. People took the movement seriously but also appreciated the power of parody and a little bit of humor, *à la* Stephen Colbert.

In this respect, Justin Bieber was the perfect person to lead the opposition, albeit unwittingly, against the copyright bills before Congress. Bieber was probably the most powerful man in the world of social media. He represented not only the possibilities of how social media and free sharing of content online could benefit society, such as by helping to discover new talent, but also the sheer strength in numbers on social media. Put simply, Bieber had followers—numbering in the millions. So, if Bieber talked, people listened.

When Congress began considering the two controversial copyright bills in 2011, it could not have foreseen how large a figure

Justin Bieber would become in the grassroots opposition against the bills. Even though his direct participation in the opposition was only minor, Bieber breathed life into the opposition in a way that no one else could. Indeed, even with Bieber's only minor involvement, the bills may well have been doomed.

*   *   *

Senator Patrick Leahy of Vermont introduced the first bill, the PROTECT IP Act (PIPA), on May 12, 2011.[1] Leahy had strong bipartisan support, with three prominent Republicans—Orrin Hatch, Chuck Grassley, and Lindsey Graham—joining Leahy and six other Democrats to co-sponsor PIPA. Senators Amy Klobuchar of Minnesota, Chris Coons of Delaware, and John Cornyn from Texas introduced a companion bill, the Commercial Felony Streaming Act (CFSA).[2]

Both bills proposed to create new enforcement measures against online piracy and counterfeiting. The bills were pitched as targeting "foreign rogue websites," meaning foreign sites engaged in copyright piracy or trademark counterfeiting.

The most controversial part of PIPA was a provision that authorized the U.S. government to engage in domain name blocking, a practice that China's government had popularized in its censorship of speech in what's notoriously called the "Great Firewall of China." That is what made the bill so controversial. PIPA would authorize the U.S. Attorney General to obtain a court order against a foreign "Internet site dedicated to infringing activities" of copyrighted or trademarked goods. The court order could instruct a search engine like Google or an Internet service provider like Comcast to prevent links and domain names of allegedly infringing foreign websites from matching up with their Internet protocol (IP) addresses—the numbers that serve as the unique address for a site so that it can be found on the Internet.[3] In effect, a U.S. court could order a foreign website to disappear from the Internet, at least for people in the United States, because the link or domain name would not match up with its IP address in the Domain Name

System (DNS) servers. Without a connection to its IP address, the domain name would be meaningless on the Internet—like a phone number that had been disconnected.

Giving the Attorney General even greater power to shut down websites scared many Internet activists. Even the most scrupulous AG might succumb to overreaching. Attorney General Eric Holder was no exception, as shown by the controversy in 2013 over the Justice Department's heavy-handed tactics in subpoenaing emails and phone records of news reporters in a leak investigation.[4]

Another section of PIPA authorized copyright holders to undertake a similar action to get a court order instructing Google, PayPal, and other Internet ad and payment providers to cut off their services to sites allegedly engaged in copyright infringement or trademark counterfeiting.[5] Unlike the U.S. Attorney General action to block domain names, the private action to cut off ad and financial services—the so-called "follow the money" approach—was not limited to foreign infringing sites. U.S. sites were fair game, too.

Senator Leahy was the second most senior senator at the time, having served for over 35 years in the Senate. He was the Chairman of the Senate Committee on the Judiciary, which, by historical practice if not logical reason, had oversight over intellectual property laws. He had been working on enacting tougher anti-piracy measures for over a year, but his first attempt—a bill introduced in 2010 called the Combating Online Infringement and Counterfeits Act,[6] or COICA for short—stalled. Not only was COICA saddled with a terrible name, but Senator Ron Wyden put a hold on the bill, a delay on considering the bill on the Senate floor, because he believed the bill would jeopardize American innovation, free speech, and the Internet.

Internet advocacy groups, including the Electronic Frontier Foundation (EFF) and Aaron Swartz's new nonprofit Demand Progress, shared Senator Wyden's concern. In late 2010, Swartz started a stop-censorship petition against COICA that collected over 300,000 signatures. A group of 50 law professors led by cyber-law expert David Post also sounded the alarm about censoring the

Internet.

The Center for Democracy & Technology (CDT) raised the additional concern that COICA's domain-name-blocking provision could have the unintended consequence of increasing cyber-security risks. David Sohn, the General Counsel and Director of CDT's Project on Copyright and Technology, who had worked for Wyden until 2005, reached out to cybersecurity expert Dan Kaminsky about the bill. Kaminsky became famous for his research in 2008 that showed a huge flaw in the Domain Name System (DNS), making it vulnerable to cyber attack. Sohn suggested to Kaminsky the idea of publishing a paper on COICA's possible threat to cybersecurity for use in the debate in Congress. Jamie Hedlund of ICANN, the nonprofit organization that oversees the DNS, approached Steve Crocker, a Board member of ICANN and one of the engineers who helped develop the first protocols for the Internet. Crocker was eager to get involved.

By February 2011, a group of five leading Internet engineers—Kaminsky, Crocker, David Dagon, Danny McPherson, and Paul Vixie, some of whom had helped to create the Internet—organized to give their technical view of COICA and to explain how it may compromise cybersecurity. Crocker, McPherson, and Vixie were all members of ICANN's Security and Stability Advisory Committee, which identifies threats to the security of the Internet. The Internet engineers hadn't been engaged with copyright policy before, but Congress was now suddenly messing with their turf.

In May 2011, the five Internet engineers published a white paper criticizing the risk to cybersecurity posed by the DNS blocking being considered in Congress.[7] Their key insight would loom large later in the debate. In July 2011, the five engineers even went to DC to present their concerns to staffers and members of Congress. They spent an entire week on the Hill because they believed Congress was about to screw up the Internet, something the engineers had helped to create and develop. As Vixie explained, "I helped build this thing. . . . This was an act of conscience for me."

Meanwhile, on September 28, 2010, during the debate over COICA, EFF's Peter Eckersley, who had a PhD in computer science and law from the University of Melbourne, submitted a letter on behalf of 87 Internet engineers to the Senate Judiciary Committee that condemned the bill and its "risk [of] fragmenting the Internet's global domain name system (DNS)."[8]

Senator Wyden's hold on COICA, which came in November 2010, effectively killed COICA's chances of passage because Congress was nearing the end of its session.

Now, in 2011, with a new Congress and an even tougher copyright bill under a catchier title—Preventing Real Online Threats to Economic Creativity and Theft of Intellectual Property Act (PROTECT IP or PIPA for short)—Leahy was determined to get its passage.

In introducing PIPA on the floor of the Senate, Leahy spoke about the importance of protecting intellectual property. "Mr. President, few things are more important to the future of the American economy and job creation than protecting our intellectual property. . . .

"Copyright infringement and the sale of counterfeit goods are reported to cost American businesses billions of dollars, and result in hundreds of thousands of lost jobs. Further, the Institute for Policy Innovation estimates that copyright piracy online alone costs Federal, state, and local governments $2.6 billion in tax revenue. In today's business and fiscal climate, the harm that intellectual property infringement causes to the U.S. economy is unacceptable."

Critics have questioned these kinds of piracy loss estimates, especially figures tabulated by the IP industry—which was the source of the figures cited by Senator Leahy.[9] To skeptics, the figures represented "copyright math," meaning overblown figures that were not based on hard data. Even the federal Government Accountability Office (GAO) questioned the methodology and accuracy of estimates of the costs of piracy and counterfeiting in an April 2010 report.[10] A basic assumption in the IP industry's estimates of its own losses caused by piracy and counterfeiting is that every unauthorized copy results in the lost sale of the product at full retail value. At least in some instances, a person who seeks to obtain a pirated or counterfeited good may be unlikely to buy the authentic good at retail value even if the illegal copies weren't available. Just think of fake Gucci bags and Rolex watches bought on the street.

In other instances, the unauthorized good may actually help to promote the artist's work and spur consumers to purchase the work and other complementary services of the artist, such as a ticket to a concert. A 2011 study of U.S. and German consumers by Columbia University's The American Assembly found that "the biggest music pirates are also the biggest spenders on recorded music."[11] In a blog post in January 2012, Cato Institute fellow Julian Sanchez would tear to shreds the methodology—or lack thereof—behind the copyright industry's piracy figures.[12]

Despite the controversy over the figures related to piracy, few, if any, participants in the political debate in the United States spoke out in favor of piracy or counterfeiting, at least not as a viable political position. In that respect, the debate in Congress was tamer than the more radical efforts of the Pirate Parties in legislatures in Europe, especially in Sweden and Germany, to reform intellectual property laws to allow, for example, unauthorized file sharing. In the United States, the debate was over how best to address copyright infringement and trademark counterfeiting, not whether to allow such activities wholesale.

In Leahy's view, PIPA would help to combat piracy. "This legislation will provide law enforcement and rights holders with an increased ability to protect American intellectual property. This will benefit American consumers, American businesses, and American jobs. . . . This bill targets the most egregious actors, and is an important first step to putting a stop to online piracy and sale of counterfeit goods."

On May 26, 2011, the Senate Judiciary Committee voted unanimously in favor of PIPA after a light-hearted, seven-minute discussion with no hearings or testimony from any experts.

The vote was not surprising and received little fanfare. However, Senator Wyden, who was not on the Judiciary Committee but again was the sole gadfly in the Senate, immediately issued a statement opposing and putting a hold on PIPA.

Wyden explained his objection: "At the expense of legitimate commerce, PIPA's prescription takes an overreaching approach to policing the Internet when a more balanced and targeted approach would be more effective. The collateral damage of this approach is speech, innovation, and the very integrity of the Internet."

Wyden's heightened sensitivity to Internet policy was perhaps shaped in part by his adolescence growing up in Palo Alto, the area that would later become the hotbed of Internet startups. But back then, the Internet really was only an idea, and Wyden, who was a star basketball player at Palo Alto High during the mid-1960s, wanted to play in the NBA. Thankfully for Internet policy activists, Wyden's NBA dream did not come true, although the Senator may have gotten some satisfaction at seeing another Palo Alto High alum, Jeremy Lin, later make a big splash in the NBA.[13]

In May 2011, Wyden was the lone dissenter in the Senate who was willing to oppose the bill publicly. Wyden would prove to be a formidable opponent of the bill, vowing in November 2011 to filibuster it until the Senate addressed the concerns he and others had raised. A filibuster—dramatized in the classic Jimmy Stewart film *Mr. Smith Goes to Washington*—allows a Senator to delay a vote on a bill simply by speaking on the Senate floor as long as he wants, unless 60 Senators vote to close debate. Wyden said he would read the names of all the people who signed petitions opposing PIPA during his filibuster, a tactic that would surely make for good theatrics. Back when the bill was introduced, however, there was no sign that Wyden would gain the upper hand.

In fact, the passage of PIPA looked like a slam dunk. By summer's end, PIPA had garnered 41 co-sponsors, or nearly half the entire Senate body, which was an unheard-of amount for bills in the Senate.[14] Senator Klobuchar's CFSA bill, which the Judiciary Committee unanimously approved by voice vote on June 16, 2011, also appeared to be coasting to easy passage.

As Congress reconvened in September 2011 from its summer recess, the House was preparing to consider a similar bill called the Stop Online Piracy Act (SOPA), which turned out to be even more aggressive in its approach. Instead of requiring a court order as would be required under PIPA, for example, SOPA allowed IP owners to proceed *directly* against Google, PayPal, and other Internet ad service and payment providers by sending the Internet service a notice alleging that one of its customers was an "Internet site dedicated to the theft of U.S. property," which was broadly worded to include sites "primarily designed or operated for the purpose of . . . offering goods or services in a manner that engages in, *enables*, or *facilitates*" copyright infringement.[15]

The problem with SOPA's wording was that nearly every digital technology that handles content could be accused of "enabling" or "facilitating" copyright infringement. For example, in its $1 billion copyright lawsuit against YouTube, which was still ongoing in 2013, Viacom accused YouTube of that exact charge: "Acting with this actual and constructive knowledge, [YouTube and Google] *enable, facilitate*, and materially contribute to YouTube users' copyright infringement, which could not occur without Defendants' *enablement*."[16] YouTube maintained, however, that it faithfully carried out its duties under the safe harbor provision of the Digital Millennium Copyright Act (DMCA), which requires Internet service providers to take down allegedly infringing content posted by their users upon receiving a DMCA notice from a copyright holder. Six long years of litigation still had not resolved the dispute—the case would still be on appeal in 2013 after the trial court had ruled in favor of YouTube.

Critics of SOPA feared that the bill would encourage even more lawsuits against new Internet platforms, which might not have the financial wherewithal like Google to survive a lengthy lawsuit. SOPA lacked sufficient procedural safeguards to prevent mistaken allegations of infringement by the Attorney General or a copyright owner against a site, which might nonetheless have to shut down due to a bogus claim. And, given the immunity from liability granted under the bills to Internet companies that simply followed a copyright holder's claim of infringement, Internet companies had little incentive to investigate or weed out bogus copyright claims.

The critics' fears of SOPA/PIPA were not unfounded if recent history is any guide. Under the Prioritizing Resources and

Organization for Intellectual Property (PRO-IP) Act of 2008, the U.S. government already has the power to seize domain names (that are registered with a U.S.-based registrar) by obtaining a warrant upon a simple showing of probable cause that the domains were involved in criminal copyright infringement or counterfeiting.[17] Afterwards, the government may seek ownership of the domain name in civil forfeiture proceedings before a court. Homeland Security's Immigrations and Customs Enforcement (ICE) has undertaken hundreds of seizures of domains in various crackdowns under the code name "Operation in Our Sites." Once a domain name is seized, the U.S. government overtakes the domain with an ominous page that warns: "This domain has been seized by U.S. Immigration and Customs Enforcement."[18]

A major problem with the Operation is that the government's domain-name dragnet appears to have swept in legitimate websites, such as Rojadirecta, a Puerto Rican site for linking to Spanish sports broadcasts, and Dajaz1, a hip hop blog. In a troubling turn of events, the feds effectively conceded they had no case in 2011, when the federal government gave Dajaz1 back its domain name. Of course, too bad the site's domain name was down for a year. And then, in a similar scenario, the federal government would later return Rojadirecta's domain name in 2012.[19] In another action called "Operation Protect Our Children," geared toward combating child pornography online, the U.S. government accidentally shut down for two days the domain mooo.com along with all of its 84,000 subdomains for various legitimate websites.[20] SOPA critics feared that SOPA would cause even greater collateral damage with the censorship of legitimate websites.

But, with the full support of Hollywood and the major copyright industries, and with bipartisan support in Congress, SOPA and PIPA appeared to have the momentum for swift passage.

To the critics of the bill, SOPA essentially doubled down on the draconian measures of PIPA—the sponsors of the bill were going "all in" with their wish list for anti-piracy measures. People feared the bills swept too far, potentially endangering basic civil liberties, including the freedom of speech and the openness of the

Internet, as Senator Wyden had warned.

That worry brought together Tiffiniy Cheng, Holmes Wilson, Nick Reville, and Dean Jansen in September 2011 for a weekend retreat to start their new nonprofit, the Center for Rights. The group of tech savvy, "free Internet" millennials met at Tiffiniy's house in the rural countryside of West Chesterfield, Massachusetts of all places, to strategize about how to stop the impending copyright bills from jeopardizing the Internet.

Western Massachusetts wasn't the likeliest of places to launch a campaign to save the Internet. But one of the marvels of the Internet is that people from the remotest parts of the country can get their message across to the world. And, with a population barely over a thousand, West Chesterfield was, by all means, remote.

Three members of the group—Tiffiniy, Holmes, and Nick—had grown up in Worcester, Massachusetts, and went to high school at the Massachusetts Academy of Math and Science, where they became good friends, drawn together by their smarts and common love of doing fun, creative things. Mass Academy was a prestigious public high school established by the state in 1992 for gifted students in their junior and senior years. The school, which was affiliated with Worcester Polytechnic Institute (WPI), had an especially strong program in math, science, and technology, but also emphasized the arts and humanities. The school even required its students to perform community service, which helped to instill in them a sense of civic responsibility.

Importantly, Mass Academy, which was connected to the university network at WPI, gave its students a pretty fast Internet connection, at least by late 1990s standards. The students were doing school projects with websites on the Internet in 1996 before most people in the United States even had Internet access. Nick helped set up a webpage that included a webcam live-streaming the view of a local street. Other students designed a local band's website that became so popular the traffic to the site nearly brought down WPI's servers. For the time, the student sites were pretty groundbreaking. They were examples of the forward-thinking, Internet-conscious education that the trio received at Mass Academy in the early days of the World Wide Web.

After high school, Tiffiniy, Holmes, and Nick did not move too far from their roots, staying mostly in the New England area for both college and the start of their careers. In 2003, the trio held a mini-reunion in Maine, taking a boat ride to the scenic Vinalhaven Island. On the boat ride, they talked about the Internet and brainstormed about the kinds of things they could build on the Internet to add to people's lives. That conversation sealed the trio's passion for doing work related to the Internet, especially to protect and build on the Internet's capacity to enhance free speech and civic engagement.

The trio decided to devote their professional careers to nonprofit work related to the Internet. They wanted to make the world a better place, but in a way that would allow them to step outside of traditional career paths and expectations. After graduating from college, they built tools for their nonprofit Open Congress to make government more open and participatory. Now, nearly a decade after their Vinalhaven boat ride, they were about to embark on one of the most important projects of their lives.

Dean Jansen was the fourth member to join the group. He had worked with Holmes and Tiffiniy at the Participatory Culture Foundation, a nonprofit dedicated to creating democratic platforms by providing open and decentralized video tools and services. Dean rode his motorcycle, a sleek, white-and-silver 2002 Buell X1, up from Brooklyn to the retreat, which served as an appetizer for his upcoming cross-country ride to San Francisco.

The four young political activists had just formed a nonprofit, the Center for Rights, in order to, as they put it, "expand the internet's power for good." The retreat marked the kick-off to planning the Center's first campaign. First order of business: coming up with a name for their campaign. They spent a good deal of time during the weekend—perhaps too much time—on their name. After shooting down several proposals, they eventually chose "Fight for the Future." "Fight" conveyed a call to action, while "future" captured the dual notions of progress and the technology of the Internet. The campaign was about fighting for progress and the Internet.

As Nick explained, "The name was about people standing up for themselves and resisting this kind of infringement of freedoms some of these corporations were pushing so vehemently. At the same time, it was about the positivity of what the Internet had created and the opportunities there. Let's not strangle this wonderful, democratizing and liberating development before it gets off the ground. It is something worth fighting for as a good thing."

After finally settling on the name, the group strategized about their first campaign. The next day was a beautiful fall day in Western Massachusetts, so the group decided to take a hike to the rolling stream at the bottom of the hill in the back of the house Tiffiniy rented. The idyllic setting in West Chesterfield, with seventy acres of an apple orchard in Tiffiniy's backyard, would prove to be a good source of inspiration for the group.

They all agreed that SOPA/PIPA was one of greatest threats to the Internet.

But how to stop it?

The campaign wasn't their first foray into Internet activism. Neophytes they were not.

In 2004, Holmes, Nick, and Tiffiniy organized the successful online protest against EMI, the copyright holder to the recordings of the Beatles' *White Album*. EMI sent a cease-and-desist letter to DJ Danger Mouse, who had made a remix recording of Jay-Z's *Black Album* and the Beatles' *White Album*, and called the remix, fittingly enough, the *Grey Album*. In the remix, which received critical acclaim, Danger Mouse used samples of the Beatles' recording without copyright permission. Paul McCartney found Danger Mouse's remix to be a tribute, but EMI owned the copyright to the recording and saw it as infringing.[21] Jay-Z was honored to have his recordings sampled, especially with the Beatles' work.[22] Although sampling was common in hip hop, U.S. courts would become skeptical of allowing unauthorized sampling under the Copyright Act, even in small amounts. As one court later put it, "Get a license or do not sample."[23] EMI threatened a lawsuit if Danger Mouse and other sites didn't stop distributing his remix album.

Danger Mouse was ready to cave in to EMI's demand. But, as

a part of a nonprofit called Downhill Battle, the trio organized a historic online protest of EMI. Nick came up with the name for the day of protest: "Grey Tuesday," which he wrote down on a scrap of paper from his bed—lest he forget the name—before he fell asleep one night while planning for the protest. "Grey Tuesday" served as the rallying cry for one of the first successful online protests.

Grey Tuesday occurred on February 24, 2004. As an act of civil disobedience, Downhill Battle encouraged websites to post the *Grey Album* on their sites, free for downloading. Over 170 sites did. And from the various sites, over 100,000 copies of the *Grey Album* and 1 million tracks from the album were downloaded that day. Following Downhill Battle's suggestion, Boing Boing and numerous other sites even turned their sites grey for the day. The protest was so big that the *New York Times*, *Chicago Tribune*, *Los Angeles Times*, *Montreal Gazette*, BBC, MTV, and other news outlets covered it. Of course, it didn't hurt to have music from the Beatles and Jay-Z involved in the controversy.

EMI eventually backed down, perhaps chastened by the negative publicity. No lawsuit was ever filed, and the *Grey Album* lived on—free on the Internet and later remixed in music videos on YouTube. Danger Mouse would go on to become a successful musician with CeeLo Green in the popular group Gnarls Barkley, as well as a producer of albums with various artists, including Beck, the Black Keys, and Norah Jones. And, in the irony of ironies, Danger Mouse signed with a music label that became a part of a joint venture with EMI.

The *Grey Album* experience would prove to be formative for Holmes, Nick, and Tiffiniy. At Downhill Battle, they learned how to organize a mass online protest against what they viewed to be the overreaching of copyright law and its harm on legitimate forms of expression. And they learned how to make a campaign go viral. Along the way, they went toe-to-toe with a major corporate copyright holder and came out on top. Not bad for a first protest. After that experience, they worked together on various other nonprofit projects, including Participatory Culture Foundation and Open Congress, which honed their skills in creating platforms and web tools to increase grassroots democratic engagement among the American people.

But stopping SOPA and PIPA was an undertaking of a completely different magnitude, a mountain versus a molehill. The group had to stop Congress and the well-heeled copyright interests of Hollywood and the entertainment industry, which had significantly more troops and more money in their war chest than a small nonprofit in Western Massachusetts.

But that did not daunt the group. At their September retreat, they settled on a strategic plan of action. They would make a video to educate people about what PIPA would do if enacted. The video had to be in terms that ordinary people could easily understand. The group immediately thought of Kirby Ferguson to develop the PIPA video. Ferguson was a writer, filmmaker, and director who created the popular video series "Everything Is a Remix," a documentary that attempts to show, using examples of famous authors and inventors like Bob Dylan and Steve Jobs, how all creativity is based on copying prior works or know-how, and transforming and combining them to create something "remixed." Kirby was a skilled creator and storyteller who knew how to convey a compelling, visually arresting message through video.

The group turned to their next agenda item. They wanted to find a compelling example that would show the overreaching of PIPA in a way that people would understand. One of the key strategic insights of the group was to focus on finding real world examples that would make the vague, complex bill more concrete—more real. The group wanted American people to see and feel what it would be like to live under the regime of PIPA and SOPA, which gave the federal government and copyright holders greater power to police the Internet. That strategic decision of simulating life under SOPA/PIPA would prove to be incredibly successful in Fight for the Future's campaign.

The group zeroed in on the Commercial Felony Streaming Act (CFSA), the bill proposed by Senators Klobuchar, Coons, and Cornyn. The CFSA would make it a crime for someone to publicly perform copyrighted works 10 or more times on the Internet without authorization during any 180-day period if (i) the total economic value of the public performances exceeds $2,500 or the total fair market value of licenses to offer performances of those works exceeds $5,000, and (ii) the infringement was committed willfully for purposes of commercial advantage or private financial gain.[24]

Victoria Espinel, the first White House IP Enforcement Coordinator, a new position created in 2009, had recommended the streaming legislation back in March 2011 in a white paper she posted on the White House blog.[25]

The Copyright Act already had a similar criminal provision against unauthorized digital copying and distribution of copyrighted content.[26] The CFSA's rationale was therefore to expand the current law's reach to the unauthorized streaming of content online, which had grown in popularity. By 2011, it was pretty easy to find illegal streaming of TV shows, movies, and sports events online. If illegal file sharing was a hydra, illegal streaming was a hydra on steroids. Cut off one head, numerous others would sprout up.

As Michael O'Leary, Executive Vice President of Government Affairs for the Motion Picture Association of America, explained in a statement to the House Subcommittee on Intellectual Property: "Streaming technology is rapidly becoming the most popular mechanism for transmitting stolen content on rogue sites. Users have instant access to illegally distributed movies and television shows without the risk or inconvenience of sometimes lengthy downloads."

However, Fight for the Future believed the language in the proposed bill was broad enough to criminalize not just streaming that Americans might find objectionable, like illegal webcasts of movies or sporting events, but also conduct that most Americans would consider innocent and socially beneficial—such as kids performing cover songs on YouTube without permission of the copyright owners. Even though such conduct may technically constitute copyright infringement, the American public would see it as a legitimate form of self-expression, not something that should be criminalized. Or so the group believed. The worry was that the government, in trying to slay the hydra, would kill the guppies as well.

After surfing through various YouTube videos, the group thought the choice for their campaign was clear: Justin Bieber.

Bieber would be their leader.

Nick was familiar with how Bieber got started on YouTube, so he floated the idea of using Bieber as the poster child for Fight for the Future's first campaign. The group watched one of Bieber's early videos from 2008, the one of him singing, as a little kid, a cover of Chris Brown's "With You."[27]

Holmes explained, "It was kind of amazing. Bieber was a prodigy. The video looks like any other random kid singing on YouTube. But it's also very good, and it's also really him singing. Bieber is creating something new. And it's interesting because you see Justin Bieber [in the video] and it's the difference between him just starting out as a regular kid and, while you are watching you know he now is this superstar. The whole thing is extremely real, authentic, kind of heart-warming, and remarkable.

"We felt we could really build a campaign around this video. Does this look like something that should be illegal? I don't think anyone could say that it should be, especially in retrospect with Bieber's success."

Nick added, "It showed how far out of line the bill was with the way that culture works, the way user culture, music culture, and creativity are working in the modern world. You would be shutting down something that self-evidently should be a part of our creative culture. On top of that, this was someone who was very much a part of the corporations that were proposing this legislation. The method they used to discover this star, they now want to make illegal—which is nonsensical. Their primary interest is control, even if it means shooting themselves in the foot."

So what was the problem? In 2007, Bieber posted 15 cover performances of various artists' works on YouTube.[28] Bieber's cover performances of established artists' copyrighted music when he was a kid probably were not authorized by any formal licenses or copyright permission. Assuming he lacked licenses, Justin's unauthorized public performances of other artists' music on YouTube could constitute copyright infringement—and, under the CFSA, potentially criminal activity. Some copyright experts might argue the activity should be protected by fair use, but no court precedent had ever decided the issue. Singing cover songs on YouTube without permission could, therefore, arguably be infringement.

But could the possible infringement satisfy the criminal thresholds under the CFSA? Possibly yes. First, Bieber's videos were incredibly popular, so there's no doubt that they were publicly performed at least 10 times in a 180-day period. Second, the cost to license a single public performance of an established artist's song could easily be in the hundreds of dollars. And YouTube videos are audiovisual works, for which copyright holders typically charge even more—potentially thousands of dollars—to license the performance of a musical work under a synchronization license.[29] Under SOPA, the House bill later introduced, the amount for criminal liability was even easier to meet at $1,000.[30]

The biggest question was whether the infringement was "committed willfully for purposes of commercial advantage or private financial gain." Mitch Glazier of the Recording Industry Association of America contended that a person making a cover video on YouTube would lack the criminal intent required for prosecution.[31] Some legal experts might argue that Bieber did not willfully commit infringement when he was only 12 years old; he probably had no idea about copyright law.

On the other hand, although willfulness sounds like a high burden to meet, under the prevailing law, a person can willfully infringe, even without knowledge that his conduct was infringing, as long as he acted in reckless disregard of possible infringement.[32] For example, the music industry successfully obtained massive statutory damage awards for willful infringement by a mother of four children and by a college student for their unauthorized music file sharing—$222,000 and $675,000 in damages for just 24 and 30 songs, respectively.[33]

And there's no doubt Justin Bieber benefited financially by signing a lucrative music deal based in part on the popularity he gained from his public performances on YouTube. In a *New Yorker* interview, agent Scooter Braun admitted that he helped Bieber's mother make some of the videos in order to build up a bigger following for Bieber to help secure a recording contract with music labels.[34] Although some legal experts might beg to differ, Harvard Law Professor Jonathan Zittrain agreed with Fight for the Future's interpretation of the bill, which, in his view, was broad enough to expose Bieber's type of activity on YouTube to potential criminal liability.[35]

At the very least, nothing in the proposed Commercial Felony Streaming Act exempted the streaming of unauthorized public performances of wannabe pop stars who performed other artists' songs on YouTube in the hopes of signing a huge record deal one day. The issue under the bill was debatable.

Of course, given how successful Bieber had become in the music industry, on top of the Constitution's bar against criminalizing completed acts *ex post facto* ("after the fact"), the chances of Bieber being prosecuted were nil. But the message of the group in using Bieber was more figurative: the bill could criminalize the same kind of activity that Justin Bieber had engaged in to become discovered. To its credit, YouTube was working to help facilitate allowing such music covers on YouTube legally. In August 2011, as a part of a settlement of a major copyright case brought against it by the National Music Publishers Association, YouTube instituted a licensing program for music publishers and composers to choose to license their musical works on YouTube and share in ad revenues. In late 2011, though, it remained unclear how many publishers would join the YouTube program and how many works would be included. Given the uncertainty, the bill could, if enacted, chill freedom of expression by discouraging kids and others from singing their favorite cover songs on the Internet.

Nick came up with the slogan to encapsulate the group's campaign: "Free Bieber."

As soon as Nick floated the name at the retreat, Tiffiniy, Holmes and Dean laughed with approval.

Free Bieber! Free Bieber! Free Bieber!

With those two simple words, the group's first campaign was born.

When the retreat ended, the group left energized and optimistic. They felt they would be able to engage the political debate—and hopefully make it really hard for their political adversaries. To some, the group's optimism might have seemed naïve or foolhardy. What chance did four individuals at a small nonprofit stand against Congress, Hollywood, the RIAA, the MPAA, media conglomerates, PhRMA, the U.S. Chamber of Commerce, General Motors, and other large corporations backing the bills?

But Tiffiniy, Holmes, Nick, and Dean saw a tremendous opportunity. No one had really organized this kind of political protest before, at least not in a systematic and sustained way. What was needed, they believed, was an organization that could put together both education and action on an issue, guided by a political strategy that could create and connect viral ideas on the Internet. The Internet was their weapon, as it were. They just needed to mobilize people through the Internet, in order to protect the Internet itself. To that end, the organization needed to have three capabilities: good political strategy, good design skills (design in the TED and Apple sense), and technical ability to build tools that people could easily use on the Internet. That's what Fight for the Future brought together.

As Holmes put it, "We thought the combination could be deadly." For SOPA, those words would prove to be prophetic.

*   *   *

On October 19, 2011, Fight for the Future launched the Free Bieber site at Freebieber.org, with the ominous header: "Justin faces 5 brutal years in prison." The site featured an amusing, Photoshopped photo of Bieber in a hoodie, standing behind bars, with fear on his face. Other edited photos showed Bieber getting arrested in handcuffs, standing in a lineup, and crying—with comical clip-art tears—in a prison cell wearing his orange prison uniform. Poor Bieber!

The site included an embedded YouTube video of Bieber's cover of Chris Brown's "With You," and explained why, in the group's view, this type of activity would become criminal under the proposed bill in Congress. The site even sold "Free Bieber" T-shirts and tattoos. The Free Bieber site asked people to sign a petition to oppose the bill. As the site explained, the only way to get Congress to listen was "sheer numbers"—mobilizing enough people to express their opposition. And that's what Fight for the Future set out to do.

The group sent out the link to the Free Bieber site to blogs, websites, and people on Facebook, Twitter, and YouTube. Philip DeFranco gave the Free Bieber site a huge boost by endorsing and linking to it in one of his videos.[36] DeFranco, who went by the username "sxephil," was a popular creator whose YouTube videos consisted of him giving commentary on current events in a manner that was kind of a cross between Andy Rooney and Jimmy Fallon. DeFranco's videos routinely received over 1 million views on YouTube, so getting mentioned in his video meant that the story commanded nearly twice as many viewers as Anderson Cooper's nightly news show on CNN.

Soon, the Free Bieber campaign began to draw the interest of the mainstream media. Getting something to go viral on the Internet is no easy task—marketers covet the possibility but rarely succeed. Fight for the Future, however, seemed to be pretty adept at creating a viral campaign. Besides the Free Bieber site, the group launched its campaign video—titled "PROTECT IP/SOPA Breaks the Internet"—on October 25, 2011.[37] Kirby Ferguson did a masterful job in putting the video together. Over the next 3 months, the video received over 4 million views and would become a key way for the group to explain its objection about the complicated bills to the American public, all in less than 4 minutes.

The *Washington Post* ran a blog post about the Bieber controversy on October 19, in an article titled "Could S. 978 Land Artists Like Bieber in Jail?"[38]

The article fairly presented both sides of the debate without drawing any conclusion. Fight for the Future was successful, though, in getting the CFSA bill framed in terms of the arresting example of Justin Bieber. The sponsors of the bill, Senators Klobuchar and Coons, had to explain to a *Washington Post* reporter why Justin Bieber would not go to jail if their bill was enacted—a question that no senator would probably ever imagine having to answer.

On that same day, one of Justin Bieber's lawyers sent Fight for the Future a cease-and-desist letter demanding that the organization stop using Justin Bieber's name, likeness, and image in their "Free Bieber" campaign. The letter contended that the organization's use of Bieber's name and image infringed his trademark and right of publicity by falsely suggesting he endorsed their group, and the letter threatened "any and all action necessary" to protect Bieber's rights. Such cease-and-desist letters are commonly used to protect trademarks and celebrity rights of publicity. Celebrities and big corporate trademark owners hire law firms to "police" their rights as a general practice. So it's unlikely Bieber himself knew about the letter or the Free Bieber site before his attorney sent out the letter.

Although no one at Fight for the Future had a law degree, letters from lawyers threatening legal action did not easily scare the group. Fight for the Future enlisted the legal representation of the Electronic Frontier Foundation (EFF), a non-profit that fights for protecting civil liberties on the Internet. Founded by Grateful Dead lyricist John Perry Barlow, EFF is a champion for protecting people's freedoms in the digital world, such as by providing pro bono legal representation to defend people from dubious intellectual property claims.

Corynne McSherry, EFF's IP Director, prepared the response for Fight for the Future on October 25 and 26, 2011. Backed with citations to relevant cases, the letter argued that the Free Bieber website's use of his name and likeness was protected free speech activity about a political issue that intellectual property law could not restrict. EFF emailed a draft to Fight for the Future to get its approval before the letter was sent to Bieber's attorneys.

The next day, October 27, turned out to be pivotal in the Free

Bieber campaign—a "Bieber moment."

Tiffiniy was reviewing the draft of EFF's response letter when something even more important came up that demanded her attention.

Back in Washington, DC, an outspoken DJ from Hot 99.5 radio named Kane was interviewing Justin Bieber on Kane's popular morning show, which was the No. 1 radio program among 18 to 34-year-olds in the DC metro area. By a stroke of luck for the Free Bieber campaign, Kane asked Bieber about Senator Klobuchar's bill. Only in DC would a copyright bill ever become a hot topic to ask teen heartthrob Justin Bieber about.

"We're in Washington, DC, and obviously we have the ear of a lot of pretty powerful people," Kane began. "There is a headline today that's talking about a brand new bill pending in Congress, about taking clips from artists and using them on YouTube and making it a felony. So if you were to sing a song by Usher—we'll use him for example since he's pretty influential in your career. If you were to use a song by Usher, sing it, put it on YouTube, you could go to jail."[39]

"Who's trying to pass this law?" Bieber asked incredulously.

"It's pending right now, and this is coming from FOX News, a senator from Minnesota is proposing a bill . . . that would make 'unauthorized web streaming of copyrighted material a felony. Illegal streaming would mean an offense that consisted of 10 or more public performances by electronic means.' So if it got played—"

Bieber had heard enough. "That guy needs to be locked up."

"Amy . . . it's a she," Kane corrected, referring to Senator Klobuchar, the bill's sponsor. "That's how you got your start—"

Bieber interrupted again. "She needs to be locked up. Whoever she is she needs to know that I am saying she needs to be locked up. Put away in handcuffs."

Kane added, "This is how Bieber got his start. You got your start thanks to YouTube. Thanks to singing other songs. That got the attention—"

"People need to have the freedoms, I mean, YouTube is a place to upload videos. People need to be able to sing songs, you know. I just think that's ridiculous."

"So you wouldn't mind if someone was to take one of your songs from [your album] *Mistletoe* or one of your original works—"

"I check YouTube all the time and watch people sing my songs," Bieber interjected. "I think it's awesome. I can see if someone is using [a copy of] my songs [recorded] in their videos or something like that. But they're singing one of my songs live?"

"Correct."

"I just think that [bill] is silly."

In less than 2 minutes, Bieber had just turned the debate over the pending copyright bills upside down.

Kane posted the clip of the interview on HOT 99.5's website with a blog post describing how "Justin Bieber Calls out A MEMBER OF CONGRESS Over So Called 'Bieber Bill.'" As is common in the age of social media, Kane allowed the audio clip to be embedded freely by others on their websites. Many did.

The *Star Tribune* in Minnesota ran a story about Bieber's comments with the audio clip.[40] CBS Minnesota ran a feature on the local news in Senator Klobuchar's home state.[41] *USA Today* and the *New York Daily News* covered the story nationally.[42]

In the blogosphere, the reaction was even more fierce. Justin Bieber fan sites picked up Bieber's criticism of the Klobuchar copyright bill. That brought a new constituency to the copyright debate: tweens and teenagers, the "Beliebers," who were all likely to be on Bieber's side.

Within the week, nearly 200,000 people signed Fight for the Future's online petition against the bill. Over 300,000 unique visitors visited the Free Bieber site. Almost overnight, Free Bieber went viral and became an Internet meme that would continue throughout the entire debate on PIPA/SOPA.

Bieber's criticism put Senator Klobuchar's office on the defensive. The Senator released a statement to quash the controversy: "Justin Bieber must have been misled about the content of this bill. It's not about people posting their personal work on the web. This is common sense legislation that passed through the Judiciary Committee with no objection from either party. The bill only covers the intentional commercial theft of things like books, commercial music, and movies, including foreign piracy."[43]

The RIAA and music publishers were even more blunt. They issued a statement attacking the Free Bieber website. "An anonymous website is hijacking a legitimate effort to protect the rights of millions of artists. Its blatant inaccuracies are unfair to all those striving to protect the rights of American creators. Senator Klobuchar's pro-artist legislation is carefully crafted to go after people who, with criminal intent, try to earn a profit from the misuse of copyrighted videos. It does not affect people who post their own videos or the services they use to do so."[44]

Neither Senator Klobuchar's nor the music industry's response was directly on point. Justin Bieber's cover videos weren't entirely his own personal videos—they contained his performances of copyrighted music of *other artists or composers.*

The Free Bieber campaign had struck a chord. In only a week after the campaign's launch, the public debate over the copyright bill was now being waged on the terms set by Tiffiniy, Holmes, Nick, and Dean as they had brainstormed near a stream in Western Massachusetts. Their campaign had now taken on a life of its own. With just a few sentences, Justin Bieber gave voice to the Free Bieber campaign in a way that no one else could.

When she heard the Bieber interview online, Tiffiniy couldn't contain herself at her home. She literally jumped up for joy! She excitedly called Holmes and Nick to celebrate the amazing news.

They had just hit the jackpot.

The turn of events was sudden and unexpected. One moment, the group was preparing to release an email revealing how they might be sued by Justin Bieber based on his attorney's letter. The next moment, Justin Bieber himself came out against the Klobuchar bill. Instead of sending the email about possibly getting sued by Bieber, Fight for the Future turned to publicizing how Bieber was on its side. The group posted the audio clip on the Free Bieber website, which started playing the audio of Bieber's interview automatically whenever anyone viewed the site.

EFF lawyer McSherry sent the reply to Bieber's attorney's

cease-and-desist letter on the same day. Bieber's attorney never responded back, which was not surprising especially given what Bieber himself had said.

One of the strengths Fight for the Future displayed during the campaign was its ability to respond quickly to any development. Within a day of Bieber's radio interview, the group launched a second site called "Bieber Is Right" that included Bieber's interview and provided commentary defending the group's analysis of the copyright bill.

Senator Klobuchar disputed Fight for the Future's interpretation of the bill, as did others who supported the bill. But the fact that people could disagree on the bill's meaning did not bode well for the Senator's position. Lack of clarity is not a selling point for any law. And without a clear, section-by-section analysis of the language of the bill, explaining why it didn't apply to Justin Bieber's unauthorized performances of cover songs performed online, the issue appeared to be at least debatable—as many issues under copyright law notoriously are.

By any measure, Fight for the Future's first campaign was a resounding success. Within just a week, the Free Bieber campaign had changed the public debate over the copyright bills. Justin Bieber's clear statement against a part of the Senate bill gave the opposition much needed momentum.

Bieber's radio interview energized the group at Fight for the Future, who found validation for their efforts in Bieber's comments.

"It shows the disconnect between somebody who really grew up with an Internet culture and corporations that are fighting to shut it down or don't have an intuitive feel for Internet culture. It is so self-evident to Bieber that you should be able to create a music cover video without permission and share it with others. It's absolutely obvious to him. Not only because he did it, but because everyone around him was doing it. It was the YouTube culture that he was a part of, and is still a part of. He's speaking from a more honest position, a more connected position than when you hear it from a corporate voice," Nick explained.

Tiffiniy was even more effusive: "It was inspiring. I felt like

I fell in love with Justin Bieber then. Bieber could have been our leader. He was expressing in terms that we couldn't say ourselves, or as eloquently as he was, what this fight was all about. He became the leader for our Free Bieber campaign."

However, the Free Bieber campaign was only the opening battle. The day before Bieber's interview, Representative Lamar Smith of Texas, the Republican Chairman of the House Judiciary Committee, introduced the Stop Online Piracy Act (SOPA) in the House. SOPA had significant support, with eventually 31 co-sponsors.[45] SOPA was even broader and more aggressive than the Senate bills in its anti-piracy provisions. And SOPA, not PIPA, would garner the lion's share of attention in the public debate going forward.

Chapter 2

American Censorship Day

With no time to savor the success of their Free Bieber campaign, the group at Fight for the Future immediately plotted their next move. Time was of the essence. Both SOPA and PIPA were going to pass this year, they feared, given all the support the bills were drawing in Congress. Internally, the group kept a "SOPA scorecard," keeping track of support and opposition to both bills. At the time, the scorecard was pretty lopsided, with far more support than opposition. It looked like a blowout.

Halloween brought an unexpected snowstorm to Massachusetts and the entire Northeast, perhaps a harbinger of things to come in Congress. The snow damaged power lines, causing outages throughout Worcester and other areas from West Virginia to Maine. Halloween festivities in Worcester were postponed for days. Children were left disappointed and cold.

Senator Scott Brown of Massachusetts, who was best known for modeling in his underwear for *Cosmo* magazine in his younger days and then eventually filling the late Ted Kennedy's seat in the Senate, tweeted the next day, "What a storm, my power is still out!"

Back in Worcester, Holmes lost heat in his house that entire week. The cold air compounded his growing worry that they were going to lose the fight against SOPA. Earlier in the week, he had taken his wife, Giseli, out to dinner to celebrate her birthday at a nice restaurant in Gloucester, only to spend part of their conversation on SOPA and fretting about how it looked like it was going to pass. Not the most romantic topic, but Holmes couldn't help but be pre-occupied with his concern over SOPA.

As he and Giseli walked around Gloucester that rainy fall evening, Holmes felt angry, if not helpless, at not being able to do anything to stop the bill. Giseli, who was well-versed in free Internet culture as well, provided a trusty sounding board. Holmes confided to her that he thought they were about to lose very big on SOPA. So he needed to come up with an idea, something to at least slow down SOPA. Or else it would be all over.

The next day, Holmes called Tiffiniy and Nick to strategize about what to do. Tiffiniy was just coming back from a walk in the snow-covered countryside of West Chesterfield to her home. The idyllic scene was a source of inspiration.

The group thought the only way to take down these bills was to organize a mass online protest of a size never seen before. The protest had to be historic, to be epic. If Fight for the Future could get millions to protest and contact their Congress members, there might be a chance to stop the bills. But the group was realistic. It would take a massive effort, something much, much bigger than Grey Tuesday or Free Bieber. And, even then, they might not succeed in stopping SOPA. It all seemed like a long shot.

The group reviewed the language of SOPA and the legal analysis by Internet non-profits EFF and Public Knowledge. What became clear to the group was that, under SOPA, Americans could wake up one day and have one of their favorite sites blocked or blacklisted by the federal government.

"That smacked of too much power, too much egregious power that gets abused and hurts innocent people and society in general," Tiffiniy lamented. Inspired by the writings of Hannah Arendt and Thomas Jefferson, Tiffiniy was the most vocal member of the group about the need to have a day of action. She wanted the group to be bold.

The trio agreed that they needed to show Americans what it would mean to have their favorite websites blocked by the U.S. government. They would build an easy-to-use tool that websites could use to censor their content on the day of protest, with a message to inform viewers how to contact Congress to oppose SOPA. Instead of websites going grey, they would go black. The more sites that censored their content in protest, the better.

As Holmes described the group's strategy, "We thought we might be able to get a few sites close to us to do it. If more sites did it, it could work really well. And if big sites did it, the sky was the limit."

The group spent time trying to come up with the right name for the campaign. Messaging was key. Just as with Grey Tuesday and Free Bieber, Nick, who had a knack for names, came up with name for the day of protest that was sure to draw attention: American Censorship Day.

People in the United States do not typically associate "censorship" with "American." It's almost a contradiction in terms. Censorship is something China does, not the United States—at least not since the forgettable days of the Red Scare in the 1920s and later McCarthyism, when the federal government targeted communist sympathizers. So would people believe SOPA was really about censorship?

Fight for the Future believed SOPA was censorship because it allowed the Attorney General to blacklist domain names and make the content of the affected websites effectively disappear—without adequate safeguards to ensure the site was criminally infringing or deserved to be shut down. Others had raised the same concern about censorship back when COICA came out in 2010. But, by October 2011, the objections to PIPA/SOPA were several, with none clearly in the lead.

Fight for the Future's decision to focus on censorship proved to be smart. The censorship theme would later resonate in the popular debate over SOPA as it progressed. The concern was raised by prominent Internet experts like Vinton Cerf, one of the "fathers of the Internet" who created its TCP/IP protocol and who now was "Chief Internet Evangelist" for Google.[1] Representative Darrell Issa, a conservative Republican from Southern California, shared the same concern. Speaking at the SOPA markup in the House

Judiciary Committee in December 2011, Issa would later criticize SOPA's imposition of duties on search engines to block links: "Once you begin to cut off links—once you become China-esque—you start a snowball effect from which there is no end." The reference was to the Chinese government's use of the same kind of DNS blocking—aka the Great Firewall of China—to censor speech. Issa, who had made a fortune from his Viper car alarm business before entering politics, was one of the first Republicans to sound the alarm about SOPA.

With no time to waste, Fight for the Future began organizing for the day of action on American Censorship Day. Holmes got in touch with Elizabeth Stark, an Internet activist who was teaching at Stanford Law School. While a law student at Harvard, she had started the Harvard Free Culture group, an organization inspired by the work of Larry Lessig and his effort to reform copyright law to accommodate people's desire to share and access works on the Internet. Although Lessig had left copyright issues to focus on the near impossible task of reforming Congress, his work and writings had inspired numerous Internet activists around the world who were carrying on the causes for an open Internet he had started. Stark had devoted her professional career to various free culture projects and founded the Open Video Alliance, a group dedicated to persuading tech companies to adopt nonproprietary, open-source video standards.

In Malcolm Gladwell's terminology from *The Tipping Point*, Stark was a connector.[2] She had numerous connections in the tech and creative artist world. They would come in handy moving forward. If Stark was the connector, the Fight for the Future activists were the mavens—people who had a special ability to communicate their knowledge to others to start word-of-mouth epidemics that go viral, in Fight for the Future's case, over the Internet. With the help of Stark, who was working pro bono, Fight for the Future's efforts began to take off—bringing in multiple actors from various fields in a coalition of forces that would prove to be unstoppable.

In speaking with Holmes, Stark suggested that Fight for the Future should reach out to artists to support the protest of SOPA.

Holmes liked the idea, so Stark set up a call with Jesse Dylan, a filmmaker who was well-versed in Internet issues, with whom Stark had collaborated in her Open Video project. He also happened to be the son of the legendary rock star Bob Dylan.

In what turned out to be a pivotal idea, Dylan suggested that they should get everybody together for a brown bag strategy session and talk to the people at Mozilla because they probably would be into the idea. Mozilla is best known for producing Firefox, the open-source web browser that draws its lineage to the now defunct Netscape. Mozilla had both a nonprofit foundation and a corporation to oversee Mozilla's products. It also had "The Mozilla Manifesto," a set of guiding principles Mozilla aspires to, so that "the Internet is developed in a way that benefits everyone." Earlier that year, both Dylan and Stark had been at Mozilla's offices for a brown bag talk by Representative Zoe Lofgren, a Bay Area native who has been a vocal critic of expansive copyright laws throughout her long tenure. Lofgren spoke against the copyright bill PIPA. The idea was to hold another brown bag at Mozilla, this time against SOPA.

Holmes didn't immediately see the benefit of having a brown bag lunch, but Stark ran with the idea. She contacted Harvey Anderson, a VP and the General Counsel at Mozilla, who was willing to host a brown bag lunch on November 9, 2011 at Mozilla's offices in Mountain View, California. Anderson had worked at Netscape in its early days back in the late 1990s when it dominated the browser market only to be overtaken by Microsoft in the browser war. After stints at several other tech companies, Anderson came on board at Mozilla in 2008 as its General Counsel. Once there, Anderson started a blog called *HJA's Blog* in which he wrote about various tech issues.

On November 9, 2011, Anderson published a blog post on SOPA that he wrote the day before, on Election Day. Anderson's blog post was pretty balanced, without overblown rhetoric. While acknowledging a piracy problem and the important need to protect IP, the post took a critical view of SOPA: "SOPA exposes intermediaries to undue financial and legal liability for content in a way that will undoubtedly chill the free flow of content and ideas embodied in both software and media."[3] It was clear Anderson already understood SOPA and the gravity of the issues at stake.

The meeting at Mozilla brought together staffers from Representatives Zoe Lofgren's and Anna Eshoo's offices, people from tech companies like Google, and individuals from nonprofits in the Internet space including Demand Progress, Center for Democracy & Technology, Public Knowledge, EFF, Fight for the Future, and the Stanford Center for Internet and Society. About 30 people attended in person, while others called in by phone.

The group met in Mozilla's open meeting space, where the company hosted a variety of talks. The room was furnished with comfortable couches and chairs, spaced in a manner that was almost ideal for watching movies. Stark and Anderson moderated the meeting.

The mood in the room was serious from the start. At a key moment in the meeting, some of the tech people from the Bay Area didn't realize SOPA had a strong chance of passing soon. Ryan Clough, a staffer from Representative Lofgren's office, informed the group that, not only did SOPA have a chance of passing in the House, *the bill will pass.*

The message was a wakeup call.

Clough explained that, given all the sponsors and lobbying groups supporting the bill already, SOPA was going to pass. The only chance of stopping the bill was for people to do something really big—and really fast.

David Grossman from Representative Anna Eshoo's office made similar comments. Others from DC who were on the call shared the same dire view.

With the update from the DC folks, the meeting attendees from the Bay Area took on a sense of urgency. As EFF lawyer Corynne McSherry described the feeling in the room, "There was a real sense of gravity, people realized it was an all-hands-on-deck moment." People in the room understood that SOPA would pass unless they did something—now.

The group agreed to create a "Stop SOPA" email list of all the various players in the growing coalition, with Ernesto Falcon, the

Director of Government Affairs at Public Knowledge (PK), taking the lead in assembling the listserv, which would eventually grow to over 125 people. If stopping SOPA would require a herculean effort, the coalition needed a way to organize and mobilize the troops.

But what would be the first plan of attack?

Other than the SOPA email list, the meeting had not produced any concrete plan for stopping SOPA.

Stark steered the meeting to Tiffiniy and Holmes, who had been mostly listening to the meeting on the phone without comment. Stark knew about their idea and was waiting for the right moment to have them propose it. That moment came toward the end of the meeting—the best idea was saved for last.

Holmes and Tiffiniy finally chimed in with Fight for the Future's proposal.

We need to have a day of action—an American Censorship Day—on which websites block their content to show people what censorship under SOPA will be like, they told the group. We can have a "censored" page pop up when a person visits a website, similar to the message the U.S. government uses when it seizes websites under Operation in Our Sites.

American Censorship Day needs to be big, so we need as many websites to join the day of protest as possible. Tiffiniy suggested that if Google could go dark for a day, the protest could have a really great impact on the SOPA debate. The focus on Google made sense from an execution standpoint. Google was the most trafficked site in the United States, so if it went black in protest, millions and millions of people would notice. But Google hadn't ever blacked out its site and hadn't ever used its home page in such a political way. So it was hard to expect Google to turn off its search engine even for a day.

The representatives from Google at the meeting let Tiffiniy's suggestion pass without comment. Earlier in the meeting, they had spoken forcefully about how bad SOPA was and how they could never again allow legislation that was so harmful to the Internet to pass, almost conceding that SOPA might pass. But the Google reps at the meeting had no authority to commit Google to a blackout, so they said nothing in response to Tiffiniy's idea.

Harvey Anderson of Mozilla liked the proposed day of action, but he thought it would be a tall order to get Mozilla to censor its entire site—meaning shutting down its business—for the entire day. As an alternative, he suggested what he called a "crazy idea" that sites could participate by blacking out just their logos. Someone from the back of the room added that they could write a script of code for websites to use to black out their logos.

Holmes thought Harvey's suggestion was a great idea and encouraged others to participate in American Censorship Day in the manner in which they felt comfortable for their sites. A blacked-out logo would still further the cause. Anderson's suggestion proved to be brilliant, as it would set the way for the likes of Google to join the even bigger Internet blackout in January 2012. Businesses would find it much easier to protest if they didn't have to shut down their sites for an entire day. But at the November 9, 2011 meeting, Google wasn't on board with committing its home page to any protest, and it didn't end up joining the blackout for the planned American Censorship Day.

The reaction in the room at Mozilla's headquarters was hard for Holmes and Tiffiniy to gauge over the phone. Few said anything.

Although they didn't reveal it at the meeting, some people were even a little skeptical of the idea. Mike Masnick of Techdirt, the leading tech blog that provided wall-to-wall coverage and criticism of SOPA, wasn't convinced an online protest would work. He worried that, if it failed, it could be a wasted effort that zapped precious time and resources from the opposition. Masnick carried a lot of weight in the tech community—his blog was a must-read during the SOPA debate, filling a void left by the mainstream media. Traffic to Techdirt doubled during that time, exploding to two million unique visitors a month. As Masnick wryly put it, "SOPA was a bad bill, but was very good for our traffic."

EFF Activist Trevor Timm, a free speech lawyer, also had concerns about the protest idea, at least its timing. Timm had spoken up at the meeting about the need to make the opposition to SOPA a fight about free speech, and he was generally in favor of a protest. But he wondered to himself if they had enough time to make the planned online protest successful with only a week left to go.

During the meeting, Tiffiniy and Holmes could not tell how many others would join American Censorship Day. Their idea might be a dud. A big dud.

By the end of the Mozilla meeting, Tiffiniy and Holmes knew that they had a lot of work left to do to get people on board. The significance of the brief discussion about American Censorship Day was not fully appreciated at the time. But it would later turn out to be one of the most important moments of the entire campaign to stop SOPA.

With less than a week to go, Fight for the Future reached out to as many of their allies as possible. Even before the Mozilla brown bag, they had secured the support of EFF, Public Knowledge, and Demand Progress, which all agreed to be co-founders of American Censorship Day. After the Mozilla meeting, the groups immediately put on a full-court press to get all of their allies on board. Free Software Foundation, Creative Commons, Participatory Politics Foundation, and other groups soon joined the fight. Anderson had not yet committed Mozilla's participation, but he sounded very interested. Mozilla would be big, if it joined. Little did Fight for the Future know that an even bigger fish in the Internet world was considering joining—Tumblr, the micro-blogging service with its millions of users, a business that Yahoo! would later acquire for over $1 billion.

The coalition went into high gear soliciting involvement from the tech community. Fight for the Future finished the website for AmericanCensorship.org, which would provide the embeddable code for websites to use to black out their logos or home pages, plus a tool to ask their readers to call or email Congress to oppose SOPA. By creating a few lines of code for people to embed in their websites, Fight for the Future would make it easy for people to join the protest. The site also included the video about the bills created by Kirby Ferguson to help explain what the SOPA debate was about.

Meanwhile, websites started joining in, left and right. The

popular social news ranking website Reddit joined, as did Masnick's Techdirt, the image-sharing bulletin board 4chan, and Boing Boing, the group blog co-edited by author Cory Doctorow. Many other smaller sites also joined the opposition, as did Brad Burnham, a venture capitalist from Union Square Ventures who was one of the first VCs, along with his colleague Fred Wilson, to speak out against SOPA.

Over the weekend, Holmes received a call from Harvey Anderson. Mozilla was in!

Harvey told Holmes that Mozilla would definitely do something to protest SOPA on American Censorship Day, and there was a chance Mozilla would be able to put a "snippet" on Mozilla's home page providing a link to Fight for the Future's website.

"That would be really amazing," Holmes said excitedly, thinking about all the traffic a link from Mozilla would generate. "Please let us know if there's anything we can do to help."

After talking with Anderson, Holmes knew things were going to be big. Real big.

When American Censorship Day came on Wednesday, November 16, 2011, the day was surreal. Back in Washington, the first day of contentious hearings on SOPA began in the House, while on the Internet thousands of websites were mobilizing to protest SOPA.

Google, Facebook, eBay, and Twitter didn't join the blackout on American Censorship Day, but they did send a letter to Congress on November 14 stating their objections to SOPA/PIPA, which the companies also published in full-page ads in the *New York Times*, *Washington Post*, *Wall Street Journal*, and *Washington Times*.[4] The next day, Rebecca MacKinnon, an Internet freedom theorist, wrote a scathing review of SOPA in a *New York Times* op-ed, "Stop the Great Firewall of America."[5]

On November 15, Stanford Law Professor Mark Lemley, rated by the *National Law Journal* as one of the 100 most influential lawyers, submitted a letter on behalf of 110 law professors to the House of Representatives. The letter, which he wrote with Professors David Post and David Levine, provided seven pages of detailed analysis of the bill and concluded that SOPA "violates the First Amendment" and "is directly at odds with the United States' foreign policy of Internet openness, a fact that repressive regimes will seize upon to justify their censorship of the Internet."[6]

On that same day, forty-one human rights and Internet rights organizations from around the world sent a similar letter to Congress stating their objections: SOPA's "use of internet censorship tools to enforce domestic law in the United States creates a paradox that undermines its moral authority to criticize repressive regimes."[7] SOPA had now begun to draw international scrutiny, given the bill's potential to interfere with the Internet. The fight over SOPA started out national, but it would soon become an international affair.

Representative Howard Berman from California, a strong ally of Hollywood, had tried to defuse the controversy. He obtained a statement from Secretary of State Hillary Clinton, who wrote in a letter on October 25, 2011 that protecting intellectual property was consistent with the State Department's Internet freedom agenda.[8] The sponsors of SOPA tried to get mileage out of Clinton's letter, but it was written in such vague terms, it really didn't help much.

American Censorship Day took off right from the start. Mozilla blacked out its logo with the words: "Stop Censorship." It also provided a link to the American Censorship Day website, sending tremendous traffic to the site.

The defining moment of American Censorship Day occurred when Holmes received an unexpected call from David Karp, the 25-year-old founder and CEO of Tumblr, which had over 28 million blogs at the time, a number that would mushroom to over 100 million in 2013.

Karp told Holmes that Tumblr was about to send a ton of traffic to Fight for the Future's website. "Are you ready?"

"Yup, we are," Holmes said, giddy with anticipation.

Karp, who started Tumblr as a "platform for creativity" when he was only 20 years old, didn't reveal to Holmes what exactly Tumblr would do. As it turned out, Tumblr's involvement would be the tsunami of American Censorship Day.

Tumblr took online protests to a whole new level.

In the most dramatic part of American Censorship Day, Tumblr completely blacked out the blog dashboard on all of its millions of blogs. So, instead of being able to write a post, Tumblr bloggers saw only blacked-out spaces covering their content. When the user moved the cursor over the blackened parts, a message from Tumblr appeared: "Congress is holding hearings today and will soon pass a bill empowering corporations to censor the Internet unless you tell them no."[9]

When Tumblr users clicked the link in the message, it directed readers to another page categorized under "protect the net," which provided further details of the protest: "As written, [the bills] would betray more than a decade of US policy and advocacy of Internet freedom by establishing a censorship system using the same domain blacklisting technologies pioneered by China and Iran."

Tumblr asked the users to enter their phone numbers and addresses to call their representatives. If they did, the website would call the users to receive a recorded message from David Karp himself describing Tumblr's talking points about SOPA, after which the website would place a call for the user to speak directly with the representative from the user's district. The set-up was ingenious.

And it worked like a charm.

By noon that day, the protest was in high gear. Tumblr tweeted that it had received 3.6 calls per second for the protest. 87,834 Tumblr users made calls to Congress, which amounted to over 1,293 hours in talk time, as estimated by Tumblr.[10]

The SOPA debate had provoked Tumblr to use its technical expertise to raise public awareness about the bill. Karp explained: "It was very clear that there was a very good chance this bill was gonna be driven through the House floor with very little input from anybody in the industry that this [bill] would have such a major effect on."[11]

Karp was referring to the fact that the House Judiciary Committee had invited to its November 16, 2011 hearings on SOPA only one witness from the tech sector—Katherine Oyama, a policy counsel for Google—and no Internet engineers at all. On the other side, five witnesses were invited to speak in favor of SOPA: Maria Pallante, the Register of Copyrights; John P. Clark, the vice president of global security and chief security officer for Pfizer; Michael O'Leary, the senior executive vice president for global policy and external affairs at the Motion Picture Association of America; Linda Kirkpatrick, the group head of customer performance integrity at Mastercard worldwide; and Paul Almeida, the president of the Department of Professional Employees of the AFL-CIO.[12]

The deck appeared to be stacked against Google from the start.

The Committee Chair, Lamar Smith, spent a portion of his opening statement on SOPA scolding Google for allowing Canadian pharmacies to advertise prescription drugs to U.S. consumers illegally, a case that Google settled with the FTC for a staggering $500 million.

"In August, Google paid half a billion dollars to settle a criminal case because of the search engine giant's active promotion of foreign rogue pharmacies that sold counterfeit and illegal drugs to U.S. patients. Their opposition to this legislation [SOPA] is self-serving since they profit from doing business with rogue sites that steal and sell America's intellectual property."

The issue was a bit more complicated than Google promoting counterfeit drugs, however. Some of the ads may have been placed on Google by legitimate Canadian pharmacies selling *genuine* prescription drugs. According to the National Association of Boards of Pharmacy, only a small percentage (1 or 2 percent) of prescription drugs in North America are counterfeit.[13] The issue of Canadian pharmacies raised a more debatable public policy issue. Some U.S. lawmakers were in favor of allowing importation of cheaper prescription drugs into the United States from Canada, an issue that played well with senior citizens living on fixed incomes. Indeed, the Senate had considered enacting a bill in 2009 to legalize the practice, an idea that President Obama had once supported as a candidate.[14] But Congress had not yet passed such legislation. So ads from Canadian pharmacies selling even genuine prescription drugs to U.S. customers were illegal. Google was in the wrong for allowing such ads, and it paid a heavy fine of $500 million.[15]

Google's Oyama received, by far, the most questions during the hearing, most of them hostile. A well-trained lawyer who had worked previously as an associate counsel and deputy counsel to Vice President Joe Biden, Oyama repeatedly stuck to the official Google line of supporting the "follow the money" approach of SOPA (i.e., cutting off financial and ad services to rogue websites) but opposing SOPA's domain-name-blocking provision. Google also sought greater procedural safeguards in SOPA to avoid collateral damage to legitimate sites.

The hearing was not a clear victory for either side. The SOPA sponsors benefited the most from the testimony of the newly-appointed Register of Copyrights Maria Pallante, who strongly supported SOPA at the hearing. Her testimony was slightly more measured, though, than her written statement, which was a ringing endorsement of the bill.

At the hearing, Pallante elaborated on domain name blocking under SOPA: "These actions require court approval and incorporate the existing legal standards of seizure and civil forfeiture law. These are the same standards that ICE has used effectively for Operation in Our Sites."

Of course, critics would take issue with Operation in Our Sites, which appeared to have taken down even some legitimate sites. Pallante's use of the Operation as a model for SOPA was a downright scary thought for critics of the bill.

Pallante testified, "Mr. Chairman, I do not want to suggest that blocking Web sites is a small step. It is not. And the public interest groups that oppose this part of the bill are right to be concerned about unintended consequences. However, it may ultimately come down to a question of philosophy for Congress. If the Attorney General is chasing 21st century infringers, what kinds of tools does Congress want to provide? How broad, and how flexible?"

As the highest official in the Copyright Office, Pallante was an important authority for the SOPA sponsors to have on their side.

Besides Pallante, O'Leary from the MPAA offered the most important contribution for the SOPA supporters during the hearing. After several Committee members questioned Oyama about why Google couldn't stop pirate sites from popping up high on Google's search results, O'Leary brought up a compelling example: a Google search of the movie *J. Edgar*, a current release only in theatres, yielded "eight pages of sites where it's free."

At least in terms of atmospherics, the example played well for the SOPA supporters. The ease of finding unauthorized movies through Google's search engine—even for the less tech-savvy members of the Committee—provided some concrete substantiation of the SOPA supporters' piracy claims. And later in August 2012, Google would bow to criticisms from the content industry and would begin to penalize, in Google search rankings, websites with high numbers of copyright infringement notices alleged against them.

The opponents of SOPA, however, also scored their points at the hearing. What became noticeable at the House SOPA hearing was the lack of any expert with Internet or computer engineering expertise who could speak about SOPA's impact on cybersecurity.

Representative Lofgren pointed out that Stewart Baker, the former assistant secretary for the Department of Homeland Security under the Bush Administration and former general counsel of the National Security Agency, had warned in an article in *Politico* that SOPA's domain name blocking would jeopardize the DNS-SEC protocol being developed, with the backing and funding of the U.S. government, to make the Internet more secure from cyber attacks. Baker had consulted with Dan Kaminsky, a leading expert in Internet security who had co authored the May 2011 white paper that first raised the DNSSEC concern. In his article, Baker warned: "Congress is getting ready to pass a copyright enforcement bill that could kill our best hope for actually securing the internet."[16]

Lofgren underscored the lack of expertise on the panel. "We've got six witnesses here; five are in favor and only one is against. And that troubles me. I'll just say that. You know, I don't think it's a balanced effort, and I'm sorry that we don't have any technical expertise on this panel in terms of engineering talent, because I think that is an important issue as to the DNS blocking portions of the bill."

That concern struck a chord with other members on the Committee, including Representatives Bob Goodlatte, a Republican from Virginia, and Sheila Jackson Lee, a Democrat from Texas, who asked questions about the issue.

Toward the end of the hearing, Representative Dan Lungren, a Republican from California, made what may have been the most effective point of the entire hearing.

"This is sort of reverse of the old story that I went to a fight and a hockey game broke out. I came here and as one who has not made up his mind on this bill, hoping to receive information on this. And I think everybody on this panel is committed to fighting piracy. . . .

"But my concern is something that was brought to my attention as the chairman of the Cyber Security Subcommittee on Homeland Security, and that is the existence of a system that has been going on for some years called DNS Security or DNSSEC. And I have heard from those—some of the engineers that have been working on this in the Internet area that if we applied this law in this way, it would undo what we've been doing to try and secure the Internet by way of DNSSEC or DNS Security.

"So, I'd like to ask the panelists if any of you feel you can speak to this point because it's one that was raised with me. . . . [T]here was some real alarm by Internet engineers, I would call them, who really don't have a dog in this fight."

Lungren, who was a former Attorney General of California, then proceeded to cross examine each witness one by one—Clark, O'Leary, Kirkpatrick, Oyama, Almeida, and Pallante. It was the only time during the entire hearing that each witness was asked the same question. None of the witnesses claimed any expertise to answer the question about DNSSEC and SOPA's impact on cybersecurity.[17] The lack of expertise was jarring.

At the hearing's end, Lungren's unanswered question loomed large, magnified by his baritone voice that carried the tenor of wisdom and intellectual heft. Lungren would not be rewarded for his important contribution to the SOPA hearing, though, as he would later become a casualty to redistricting and lose reelection in 2012 by a mere 5,700 votes.

Meanwhile, outside the hearing, American Censorship Day was in full swing.

Representatives Lofgren and Eshoo joined the protest by blacking out their websites in opposition to SOPA. Eshoo also sent a letter on behalf of herself, Lofgren, and nine other representatives to Committee Chair Smith, the sponsor of SOPA, and to Representative John Conyers, the ranking member of the Committee.[18] Lofgren was successful in getting Republican presidential candidate Ron Paul—a favorite among libertarians and the Tea Party—to sign the letter after she told him about how bad the bill was during a chance encounter with Paul on the House floor. The letter expressed support for the goal of combating piracy but warned that SOPA had "overly broad language … [that] would target legitimate domestic websites, creating significant uncertainty for those in the technology and venture capital industries."

Back at Fight for the Future, Holmes worked into the evening preparing an infographic to highlight on websites the huge success of American Censorship Day.

When the dust settled on American Censorship Day, Fight for the Future reported that over 6,000 websites had participated in the protest and 2 million people signed the online protest against the bills.[19] The American Censorship Day site itself received over 1.6 million unique visitors.

And over 1 million contacts, including over 80,000 phone calls, were reportedly made to Congress that day, in large part thanks to Tumblr. To put that number into perspective, most run-of-the-mill legislation might not generate even 100 calls or messages total from constituents to a Congress member's office. The SOPA/PIPA bills had eclipsed that mark in one day, many times over. Even with all the advances in Internet technologies, simple phone calls had the surest impact on Congress. As Representative Lofgren advised the stop-SOPA coalition, "You need to melt the phone lines."

When Ernesto Falcon from Public Knowledge heard the numbers of people who got involved in the protest, he thought for the first time the coalition was winning this fight. Falcon, who had worked as a congressional staffer and still had many connections in Congress, understood that numbers mattered on the Hill. With so many people signing petitions and contacting their Congress members, Falcon knew they had a movement.

*   *   *

All in all, American Censorship Day exceeded the coalition's wildest imagination. The day had burned a hole in SOPA, changing the terms of the debate.

The next day, Representative Nancy Pelosi, the former House Speaker, expressed her reservations about SOPA, fittingly enough, on Twitter. On November 3, 2011, Jeffrey Rodman, the co-founder and "chief evangelist" of videoconferencing company Polycom, wanted to get Pelosi's view on SOPA, so he tweeted her a question: "Where do you stand on Internet censoring and #SOPA?"

A week later, right after American Censorship Day, Pelosi surprisingly tweeted back a response: "Need to find a better solution than #SOPA @DontBreakTheInternet."[20]

Rodman didn't expect a response from Pelosi, so he was floored when he read it on Twitter. He understood the significance of the reply and immediately retweeted it. Others did too—over 500 times. When he saw the number of retweets, Rodman told his wife he was getting his fifteen minutes of fame, on Twitter of all places.

Pelosi's short tweet was monumental. The tweet signaled the tide had turned on SOPA. It was no longer a done deal.

In fact, SOPA's chances of passage were tumbling downward, in large part due to Tumblr. Looking back on American Censorship Day's success, Tiffiniy underscored the importance of Tumblr's involvement. Tumblr provided the "Bieber moment" of American Censorship Day.

Tumblr was a company with millions of users, meaning the protest had reached beyond the nonprofit world and beyond media journalism sites. It had reached a corporation that put out a product and service for millions of people. That was a defining moment for the American Censorship Day protest—one that would foreshadow the importance of Google's later involvement in the even bigger mass protest of SOPA in January 2012.

The next day, the EU Parliament even passed a resolution with a thinly veiled warning to the United States against the passage of SOPA, "stress[ing] the need to protect the integrity of the global internet and freedom of communication by refraining from unilateral measures to revoke IP addresses or domain names."[21]

The success of American Censorship Day made Tiffiniy feel, for the first time, that the opposition to SOPA had a realistic chance of succeeding. And the opposition now had a blueprint for how to mobilize a successful mass protest online. Now they only needed to finish what they started.

That night, Holmes changed into his "Free Bieber" shirt so he could proudly wear it in public. Holmes went out with his wife, daughter, and friends to dinner at a local bar in Worcester. Most of the patrons probably had no idea what he and Fight for the Future were doing, or how important they were to the growing coalition against SOPA in Congress. But the day's successful protest was enough recognition for Holmes.

The Free Bieber campaign seemed ages ago, but Holmes could not help but reminisce about it that night. Wearing his Free Bieber shirt, he felt really good about the organization he and his friends had started, and extremely proud of what they had accomplished in only two short months.

As Holmes put it, they had done something significant. Something real. Justin Bieber just may be saved, after all.

Chapter 3

Bring in the Nerds

American Censorship Day signaled a major victory for the grassroots movement, which drew together various tech companies, Internet nonprofits and activists, bloggers, and everyday Internet users. The movement was growing, if not exploding, from the bottom up. No single person or entity was in control. The stop-SOPA campaign had now taken on a life of its own.

Soon, SOPA began to seep into the mainstream media. Though none of the nightly news programs on the major television networks covered American Censorship Day, the next week both the *Los Angeles Times* and *The New York Times* ran editorials against SOPA as a threat to free speech and the open Internet.[1]

Stephen Colbert soon got into the mix. He ran a hilarious segment on SOPA on his show on December 1, 2011.[2] To his credit, Colbert was the first among the TV media to discuss SOPA at any length. Colbert, whose show was owned by Comedy Central (a subsidiary of Viacom, which supported SOPA), loved to preach on the show about the need for protecting copyrights and how he, as a media provider, wanted to stop piracy. On previous episodes, he sparred with the likes of Larry Lessig and EFF co-founder John Perry Barlow about copyright law. Like no one else could, Colbert made strong copyright enforcement, especially for his show, sound cool.

On the December 1st episode, Colbert decried, in his inimitable way, counterfeiting and digital piracy—pointing to the "shocking number" provided by the FBI of $200 to $250 billion in losses to U.S. businesses due to counterfeiting. A moment later, Colbert ironically pointed out that "FBI officials . . . [have] no record of source data or methodology for generating the estimate and that it cannot be corroborated."

"That's what happens when the FBI buys bootleg reports off a card table in Chinatown," Colbert lamented.

In touting SOPA, Colbert said in a stern tone: "We will bring swift and sure justice to hardened criminals on YouTube." The screen then cut away to a YouTube video of three teenage girls singing and dancing goofily to Beyonce's recording of "Single Ladies."

The scene was deliciously ridiculous in its portrayal of SOPA. The girls probably didn't have a copyright license to use Beyonce's recording in their video, so the streaming of the recording online could expose them to the criminal streaming part of SOPA that was the equivalent of the Commercial Felony Streaming Act, aka the "Bieber bill," in the Senate.

Later on the show, Colbert held a roundtable of sorts on SOPA. Music industry executive Danny Goldberg defended SOPA. Colbert used kid gloves on Goldberg, who spoke about the need for "the pendulum . . . to swing back to the middle" to allow copyright holders to police theft of their works online.

"Can we get some Internet policemen, maybe those guys from *Tron* on motorcycles?" Colbert quipped.

Colbert then turned to Harvard Law Professor Jonathan Zittrain, whom Colbert seemed eager to go after. "Joining us now to defend thieves and pirates, please welcome professor of Internet law at Harvard: Jonathan Zittrain."

The audience laughed and applauded.

Zittrain was a computer and Internet whiz, with spectacles and boyish looks that fit the part of professor/tech geek perfectly. In 1998, only a few years out of law school, Zittrain co-founded the Berkman Center for Internet and Society at Harvard, a think tank that brings together leading theorists and activists to work on Internet-related projects.

"Why do you want artists to starve?" Colbert asked inquisitorially.

"I want artists to thrive," Zittrain replied assuredly, though he was really nervous inside. Although he had been on *The Colbert Report* once before and came out unscathed, Zittrain knew how sharp Colbert was in interviewing (read: skewering) guests. Colbert could turn even the smartest of guests into silly putty.

But Zittrain was ready with a response. "The Internet allows artists to find their audiences. When Justin Bieber started just singing his favorite songs on YouTube, he got discovered, thanks to the Internet. The odd thing is, under this law, SOPA, the behavior of Justin Bieber—singing his favorite songs, without authorization over the Internet—"

"Yes, I understand," Colbert interjected, growing impatient.

"Could make him a felon in jail for three years."

The audience burst into applause.

"Excuse me, excuse me, excuse me!" Colbert admonished the audience. "Clap after I nail him." Colbert then retorted, "Are you saying you do not want to see Justin Bieber in jail?"

"Not for this," Zittrain said with a wry smile.

That line brought more thunderous applause from the audience, who clearly sounded sympathetic to Zittrain's position.

The Free Bieber meme, devised by a small group of free speech activists from Massachusetts, now had infiltrated *The Colbert Report* on national TV. Zittrain had seen the Free Bieber site before coming on the show and picked up on its meme. And it resonated with the audience. Even Colbert seemed disarmed. Fight for the Future had scored another victory.

*　　*　　*

Darrell Issa and Ron Wyden couldn't be on further ends of the political spectrum.

Issa was a conservative Republican from Southern California. On the hot-button issues like abortion, gun control, and taxes, Issa was as conservative as they come. He also developed a name for himself by standing up to the Obama White House. Indeed, the

White House may have anticipated that Issa would become a gad-fly even before he assumed the Chair of the House Government Reform and Oversight Committee in 2011. A book by *New York Times* reporter Mark Leibovich claimed that a White House dep-uty press secretary tried to get reporters to check into Issa's past, while the Democratic Congressional Campaign Committee circu-lated negative information on Issa, in order to thwart his bid for Chair.[3] The White House efforts failed. Issa became Chair of the Oversight Committee, and he soon clashed with President Obama and Attorney General Eric Holder over a host of issues.

Wyden, by contrast, was pro-choice, pro-gun control, and a pretty moderate Democrat. Being from Oregon, Wyden had an independent streak, though. A respected expert in health policy, he teamed up with conservative Republican Paul Ryan to write a proposal to reform Medicare that the Obama Administration op-posed. However, after Ryan became Mitt Romney's VP selection, Wyden had to distance himself from a similar Medicare reform plan Romney and Ryan proposed. Wyden said his earlier plan with Ryan was premised on a Medicare guarantee.[4] But Wyden's stance on Obamacare was a complicated one. Although Wyden voted in favor of Obamacare, he was instrumental in getting a waiver for states to opt out of the federal plan if they meet certain require-ments starting in 2017.[5] Wyden would even propose some changes to Obamacare in 2013.[6]

Despite their differences, Issa and Wyden were kindred spirits when it came to the Internet. They both believed in a free and open Internet, and both were skeptical of government regulations of the Internet. Along with Republican Representative Christopher Cox, Wyden, then in the House, co-authored Section 230 of Commu-nications Decency Act, which provides immunity for Internet Ser-vice Providers from liability (except intellectual property liability) based on the content of their users. Section 230 has become one of the most important protections for Internet companies. Wyden and Cox also co-sponsored the Internet Tax Freedom Act of 1998, which bars discriminatory taxes on Internet activities. Some believe the Act helped spark the tremendous growth of e-commerce. Issa, who made a fortune in consumer electronics—indeed, he was the wealthiest member of Congress in 2011, with a net worth of over $451 million—had a natural affinity for technology and the Internet.

In 2011, the controversial copyright bills PIPA and SOPA brought Wyden and Issa together in their vocal opposition to the bills. On December 8, the two legislators unveiled their alternative bill called the Online Protection and Enforcement of Digital Trade (OPEN) Act. Never mind that the acronym doesn't exactly work. Issa and Wyden proposed a beta version of the bill, as it were, on their site, Keepthewebopen.com, which allowed the public to make comments and suggestions to improve the bill through crowdsourcing.[7]

The OPEN Act was different from SOPA/PIPA in a couple key respects. The OPEN Act didn't authorize any DNS blocking by the government, so the most controversial provision of SOPA/PIPA was gone. And the Act required IP rights holders to file a proceeding before the International Trade Commission (ITC) to seek the shutting down of ad or payment services to allegedly rogue sites. The ITC already hears many "Section 337" complaints brought by U.S. patentees to block imports of allegedly infringing goods in expedited proceedings that last a little over a year. Unlike SOPA, the OPEN Act would require the ITC to investigate and evaluate claims by IP owners before requiring any shutting down of ad or financial services to Internet sites. And the accused websites would have an opportunity to be heard before the ITC could issue a shut down of any services.[8]

*   *   *

Meanwhile, the SOPA sponsors were gearing up for the mark-up of the bill in mid-December 2011. The strategy was to get the bill voted on and passed by the Committee, at which point the full House could take a vote on the bill at any time. With the upcoming holiday recess, that would likely mean some time in January 2012.

The opposition to SOPA got a boost from Harvard Law

Professor Laurence Tribe, one of the most respected constitutional law scholars in the country, who wrote a legal memo against SOPA on December 6, 2011.[9] The memo explained why, in Tribe's view, SOPA would violate the First Amendment. Tribe's memo offered a point-for-point response to a letter written by veteran First Amendment lawyer Floyd Abrams, who argued that SOPA was perfectly consistent with the First Amendment as a measure to stop copyright infringement.[10] Tribe and Abrams were hired by opposing sides in the SOPA debate, but the two legal experts' analyses still carried weight. Marvin Ammori, a rising First Amendment lawyer who graduated from Harvard Law School, also got into the fray with a detailed memo against SOPA.[11] The battle of First Amendment experts didn't have a clear winner, but Tribe's and Ammori's withering critique of SOPA added legal credibility to the claims of the SOPA opposition.

On the night of December 12, 2011, Chairman Smith posted a manager's amendment to the SOPA bill online. The amendment attempted to address some of the criticisms raised against SOPA. The biggest change was to require a court order before a copyright holder could require financial and ad service providers to terminate their service to a suspected rogue site. So, instead of a notice-and-shutdown process that took place outside of court, the amended bill would require a court's involvement.[12]

The manager's amendment also narrowed the scope of the term "Internet site dedicated to the theft of U.S. property" in several critical ways. First, it removed the controversial "enables" or "facilitates" part that could have exposed even legitimate Internet platforms to liability. It also required the accused site to be engaged in copyright infringement "for purposes of commercial advantage or private financial gain, and with respect to infringement of complete or substantially complete works." Finally, it limited the accused websites under SOPA to *foreign* websites.[13]

But the most controversial provision of all—DNS blocking— still remained largely intact. The manager's amendment took out a specific provision that required Internet services to "prevent the domain name of the foreign infringing site (or portion thereof) from resolving to that domain name's Internet Protocol address." But the amendment still required that "[a] service provider shall take such measures as it determines to be the least burdensome, technically feasible, and reasonable means designed to prevent access by its subscribers located within the United States to the foreign infringing site that is subject to the order."[14] That vague requirement could—and probably would—require DNS blocking to carry out a court's order to disable access to a foreign site. Indeed, the "safe harbor" offered to Internet services under SOPA specifically contemplated DNS blocking as the surest route to the safe harbor from liability.[15] As Representative Lofgren pointed out at the markup, the safe harbor seemed to create a "back door way" to require DNS blocking.[16]

To complicate matters even further, the manager's amendment offered a so-called "kill switch" that would enable an Internet service to refuse to comply with a court order if it "would impair the security or integrity of the domain name system."[17] The kill switch seemed in tension with the safe harbor: if domain name blocking was inherently harmful to DNS security, as numerous experts warned, then it was difficult to see how an Internet service could avoid impairing security while falling within the SOPA safe harbor. The mechanics were unclear, if not contradictory. The manager's amendment punted the hard details on DNS blocking to the courts and parties to hammer out. Domain name blocking still was a live issue under SOPA.

With that 800-pound gorilla still occupying the room, the bill's markup was bound to be contentious. And it was.

The manager's amendment threw Representative Lofgren's office into a frenzy. They had only a couple days left before the markup, not only to digest the manager's changes, but also to revise all of their own amendments so that they would match up with the amended SOPA bill. Ryan Clough, Lofgren's legislative counsel, spent the next 48 hours reworking all of Lofgren's proposed amendments. Clough worked into the night, managing to get only a couple hours of sleep during the two-day period. But he got the work done by the deadline, though barely.

On December 15, 2011, the House reconvened its SOPA hearing for the markup of the bill to entertain a long list of over 60 proposed amendments to the bill. By then, the opposition to SOPA was growing, even in the Committee. Many of the amendments were offered to address at least some of the growing objections to SOPA, for example, by narrowing the scope of the bill or providing greater procedural safeguards.

Reddit, the news-linking social network, put a link on its home page to the live stream of the markup from the House Judiciary Committee website. Reddit's link helped to drive a great deal of traffic to the Judiciary Committee website, making the markup one of the most watched in recent memory. It was a spectacle.

At the start of the markup, Chairman Smith warned, "As far as this markup goes, it is not likely to be one of our shortest markups, and so I encourage members to bring their lunch and a flashlight. We will probably go late tonight and go tomorrow as well."

He was not kidding.

The markup got off to a slow start after Lofgren objected to the waiving of the reading of the manager's amendment. The objection was unusual. On most occasions, the formal reading of a bill is waived after the clerk reads the title of a bill. Reading a bill aloud in its entirety is only a tad less tedious than reading a phone book.

But Lofgren objected this time, explaining, "The public doesn't even know in many cases what's in this amendment. . . . I think just in the interests of transparency for the public, we ought to have an airing of what is in this manager's amendment. . . . I am mindful in the 1990s, when I was a member of this committee when we formatted the DMCA, we spent years. I mean, hundreds of hours working on this measure. This is being jammed through in 2 months' time. So I do object to waiving the reading of the amendment."

That meant the clerk at the Hearing, Sarah Kish, a professional staffer for the Judiciary Committee who was only a few years out of college, had to read every word of the proposed manager's amendment to SOPA—all 71 pages of it. The reading lasted over an hour, even though Kish read the bill very quickly. When she finished, the Committee members applauded. Representative Lofgren jokingly moved to have her receive a raise for her tireless reading.

That would be the only light-hearted moment during the entire markup.

Chairman Smith and Ranking Member Conyers began the markup by giving their opening statements, which strongly endorsed the revamped SOPA in the manager's amendment. Conyers, a Democrat from Detroit, had served in the House for 46 years, making him the second most senior member of the House. At the end of his statement, Conyers had a warning for his fellow Committee members who might be hoping to stall the bill.

"[I]f you want 65 amendments to be debated and voted up and down, fine. I plan to be here no longer than the House is in session, which mercifully will come sooner rather than later. So I am ready to go next year, next month, and any time that it takes. If somebody thinks that a bill of this magnitude is going to be stalled because we get tired, they got the wrong thing coming."

Representative Goodlatte, Chairman of the Subcommittee on Intellectual Property, Competition, and the Internet, also endorsed the manager's amendment. But he acknowledged some problems with the bill and said he hoped the markup would address them.

Mel Watt, a Democrat from North Carolina and Ranking Member of the Subcommittee on Intellectual Property, was the final person to deliver an opening statement. It was a doozy.

"From my perspective, just as an old country boy, and, you know, this is the only way I can understand this complex stuff, we need parallels in the virtual world to what we have in the real world. And I think this bill draws the appropriate balance to get us into that space."

Watt's folksy opening remarks made their way onto YouTube—for roasting.[18]

Representative Lofgren spoke against the bill. "If this bill passes with the mandate for domain name and other Internet filtering intact, I think it will be historic, and not in a good way. I don't think they will be going back. I think once the government has a taste of this power, the temptation to exert an ever-greater amount of control over the Internet through filtering technology will be irresistible."

Representative Jim Sensenbrenner, a Republican from Wisconsin who had yet to stake out his position on SOPA, followed Lofgren with an equally strong statement opposing SOPA. Sensenbrenner was a former Chairman of the Judiciary Committee and had been in office for 32 years, so his opposition brought tremendous clout to the opposition of SOPA. Sensenbrenner elevated the objection about cybersecurity to an issue of national security—which would prove to be an Achilles heel of the SOPA sponsors.

With Sensenbrenner joining the opposition, the fight over SOPA was on.

What transpired over the next day and a half was nearly 14 hours of nonstop discussion about various SOPA amendments. The first day alone was a marathon session lasting 11 hours. Chairman Smith even called in for pizza to feed the hungry Committee members. The discussion at the markup was often contentious. Amendment after amendment proposed by the critics of SOPA was discussed, and shot down.

Far from being open to compromise, the sponsors of SOPA appeared to be digging in their heels. They rejected nearly every amendment that was offered to provide more due process to protect against erroneous claims. EFF live-tweeted the entire markup, while Techdirt live-blogged it. The hearings were a complete spectacle, in a frightening way.

The most salient aspect of the markup was the Committee's lack of technological knowledge about the Internet, which was on full display during the debate. As *Washington Post* writer Alexandra Petri put it, the markup was like "a horrifying dream that a group of well-intentioned middle-aged people who could not distinguish between a domain name and an IP address were trying to regulate the Internet."[19]

Representative Jason Chaffetz, a 44-year-old Republican from Utah, sounded the same warning to his fellow Committee members, most of whom were much older than he. "This is the wrong remedy. . . . Basically, we're going to do surgery on the Internet, and we haven't had a doctor in the room tell us how we're going to change these organs. We're basically going to reconfigure the Internet, and how it's going to work, without bringing in the nerds, without bringing in the doctors. Again, I worry that we did not take the time to have a hearing to truly understand what it is we're doing."

The "nerds" became a meme during the hearing, as several legislators on the Committee proudly confessed not being "nerds," or not being equipped to speak on the technical aspects of the Internet—as if ignorance was bliss.

In January, Jon Stewart would later roast the Committee on *The Daily Show*: "Really? . . . Nerds? You know, I think actually the word you're looking for is experts. To enlighten you so your laws don't backfire and break the Internet."[20]

At the markup, Chaffetz challenged: "To my colleagues I would say, if you don't know what DNSSEC is, you don't know what you're doing."

Dr. Leonard Napolitano, Sandia National Laboratories' director of computer sciences and information systems (who was also Homeland Security Director Janet Napolitano's brother), echoed the same concern about DNSSEC in a key letter to Representative Lofgren in November 2011.[21] Then, on the day of the markup, a group of 87 Internet engineers led by Vinton Cerf sent Congress a letter organized by EFF that warned: "Censorship of Internet infrastructure will inevitably cause network errors and security problems. This is true in China, Iran and other countries that censor the network today; it will be just as true of American censorship."[22]

Not even the Committee's staunchest supporters of SOPA were willing to dismiss the cybersecurity concerns. To make the Internet more vulnerable to cyber and possibly terrorist attack played well on neither side of the aisle.

However, Goodlatte, a Virginia Republican who was a leader in tech issues for his party, was prepared to counter the formidable challenge to SOPA raised by the cybersecurity experts. Goodlatte submitted into the record written statements of three experts—George Ou, a senior analyst at the Information Technology & Innovation Foundation (ITIF) and also an IT and information systems security consultant; Daniel Castro, another senior analyst at ITIF; and Richard Bennett, an ITIF Senior Research Fellow specializing in broadband networking. The three experts disagreed with the analysis that domain name blocking posed a cybersecurity risk that would undermine DNSSEC. ITIF, a nonprofit think tank based in DC, was one of the first to float some of the ideas underlying SOPA, such as blocking websites, back in 2009. The paper was provocatively titled "Steal These Policies: Strategies for Reducing Digital Piracy."[23] So it was not surprising that ITIF's analysts were now trying to defend SOPA.

Castro's white paper argued that SOPA did not require DNS redirection, but instead gave Internet service providers several options that would not frustrate DNSSEC, including the possibility "that a DNSSEC server can simply decline to resolve an IP address for a domain name of a foreign infringing site by not responding to queries for that domain name." Castro also argued that policymakers should consider how DNSSEC could be developed in conjunction with other goals, including reducing piracy.[24] Castro didn't believe that a group of Internet engineers should be foreclosing the policy debate simply by developing Internet protocols.

Goodlatte scored some points for the sponsors of SOPA by providing, for the first time, the statements of several IT experts to respond to the intense criticism of SOPA from many Internet engineers.

However, Lofgren pointed out that the three IT experts Goodlatte relied on were all funded by the movie industry. "To say that three people who were funded by an interested party is the equivalent of the entire Internet world in terms of engineers and scientists is preposterous. Yes, there is a controversy, but the controversy is why we would listen to people who have been paid to say something that is wrong in the face of the entire Internet science world saying this is a catastrophe."

Lofgren made a decent point, especially about the many disinterested Internet engineers opposing SOPA. The funding issue was more debatable, however. Although ITIF received a general contribution of $25,000 from the Motion Picture Association of

America in 2010, as a nonprofit ITIF didn't accept money specifically to fund the writing of its position papers (as was more common for legal experts, including Professor Tribe and Floyd Abrams, both of whom were retained to write their dueling memos on SOPA).[25] As it turned out, a number of tech companies that were against SOPA, including Google, had also contributed to ITIF in the past.[26]

Lofgren also submitted a formal refutation of Castro's paper from the five Internet engineers who wrote the original May 2011 white paper that had first sounded the alarm about how DNS blocking under the proposed bills posed a threat to DNSSEC and cybersecurity. The Internet engineers disputed Castro's claim that a DNS server could simply decline to respond to a query for a domain. "This well-intentioned proposal ignores the fact that a secure application expecting a secure DNS answer will not give up after a timeout. It might retry the lookup, it might try a backup DNS server, it might even start the lookup through a proxy server. Since there is no way a secure application can know whether a timeout is due to a national anti-piracy law, it will have to assume the worst, which is: that it is under attack."[27] Behind the scenes, some of the Internet engineers took umbrage with Castro's expertise as an IT specialist who had no experience in Internet engineering. If Castro proposed to change DNSSEC, why didn't he help to develop such a protocol or at least offer a proposal at an open forum of the Internet Engineering Task Force?

Despite Goodlatte's best efforts to put to rest the cybersecurity issue, it loomed large throughout the markup. If numbers meant anything, the weight of authorities appeared to be against SOPA as a threat to DNSSEC and the ongoing efforts to improve cybersecurity in the United States. Granted, three IT experts disagreed with that concern as overblown and off-base, but scores of Internet engineers had at least raised a serious question about SOPA's effect on cybersecurity. The disagreement among the experts only underscored the lack of testimony at the hearing from *any* experts—the so-called "nerds"—on either side.

Lungren, who had stolen the show at the November 16, 2011

hearing with his effective cross-examination of the witnesses on this very issue, summed up the gap in testimony the best.

"We are being asked to pass fundamentally important and changing legislation with respect to the operation of important parts of the Internet without the information base I think that we need, and I would agree with my friend, the gentleman from Virginia [Goodlatte], that we won't become the technological whizzes by having experts here, but it will give us a better base upon which to make a judgment. . . .

"And I know we have two or three people saying that the DNS blocking is not going to affect our ability in protecting cybersecurity, the operation of the Internet, but we have got a whole slew of people on the other side, and I just know from my perch in the cybersecurity arena, they are warning me that we ought not to take this step."

Seizing on Lungren's remarks, Sensenbrenner and Issa suggested that the proper course would be to schedule a hearing after the holiday recess so the Committee could hear from Internet engineers. Watt objected, though, expressing skepticism that a battle of the experts in Committee would educate them any more on the issue.

Maxine Waters of California had heard enough. Irritated by the slow pace of the markup, which she attributed to the opponents of SOPA, Waters asked Chairman Smith to tell the rest of the members who were trying to slow down the markup that he would not put off the proceeding.

Chairman Smith remarked, "Yes, I have every intention of going forward today, tomorrow, and however long it takes."

Smith tried his best to carry out his promise, but he finally— and unexpectedly—relented in the middle of the second day of the markup, which was proceeding at a snail's pace, with many of the proposed amendments still left to consider. But the day was the last of the session, and the members had votes upcoming on the floor, plus flights out of DC later that day. Smith ran out of time.

In the end, the opponents of SOPA in the Committee were successful in delaying a vote on the bill in the markup. A vote delayed was a bill denied.

Smith postponed the markup until the "next practicable day that Congress is in session." That meant later in January 2012, given the upcoming recess. Smith even expressed a willingness to consider holding a hearing on the cybersecurity issues raised. But, before Smith could reconvene the Committee, even more dramatic events would overtake the SOPA debate in January 2012.

*　　*　　*

GoDaddy is a domain name registrar and website hosting service best known for its Super Bowl commercials featuring scantily clad "GoDaddy girls," including racecar driver Danica Patrick. GoDaddy liked to push the envelope with its racy advertising, but, when it came to SOPA, it fell right in line with other corporate supporters of the copyright legislation when it was first introduced.

GoDaddy's support of SOPA did not sit well with many of its customers who owned websites or domain names hosted by GoDaddy. Websites owners, not surprisingly, disliked the government's intermeddling with the DNS and the Internet.

In December 2011, one customer wrote a letter to GoDaddy to terminate GoDaddy's service and transfer all 51 domain names the customer had at GoDaddy to another host due to GoDaddy's support for SOPA. Under the username "selfprodigy," the irked customer even proposed on the social news site Reddit that other GoDaddy customers join in a protest of GoDaddy on December 29.[28] The post received over 37,000 "up" votes, causing the item to bubble up to the top of Reddit's home page. So eager were Reddit users—so-called Redditors—for the protest, the date was moved up to December 22 and would extend for at least a week.

Clearly, the Reddit community didn't like SOPA. Reddit, which was owned by magazine media giant Conde Nast, had retained its independence in operations. That allowed it to continue to provide a no-holds-barred forum for its users.

Reddit's General Manager, Erik Martin, and its programmers were troubled about SOPA, but didn't know exactly what to do.

Martin believed in the wisdom of the Reddit community, so he crowdsourced the SOPA issue to Redditors, all 28 million of them. In December 2011, Martin decided to make SOPA a prominent issue on Reddit's home page, with a direct link to the SOPA forum. That's where the GoDaddy protest was born.

The GoDaddy protest received incredible momentum after Ben Huh, the CEO of the popular comedic Cheezburger network, tweeted: "We will move our 1,000 domains off @godaddy unless you drop support of SOPA. We love you guys, but #SOPA is cancer to the Free Web."[29]

Huh's network of 51 sites commanded over 340 million page views a month, so GoDaddy would have been well-served to treat the impending protest with the greatest of urgency.[30]

Instead, GoDaddy initially released a statement saying that it had "not seen any impact to our business" from the boycott.[31]

By the end of December 23, 2011, however, GoDaddy's tune changed. CEO Warren Adelman dropped GoDaddy's support for SOPA like a hot potato. "We can clearly do better [than SOPA]. . . . Go Daddy will support it when and if the Internet community supports it."[32]

By then, the damage was done.

Over 37,000 domain names had been transferred from Go-Daddy—a number that mushroomed to over 70,000, including several hundred of Wikipedia's domains, in the final aftermath.[33]

The Reddit community had become a force in the SOPA debate. The fervor against SOPA in the Reddit community had become fierce, just as strong as a mother's love for a child. To borrow the words of Agatha Christie: "It dares all things and crushes down remorselessly all that stands in its path."[34] Martin's and Reddit's tremendous influence would later be recognized by *Time* magazine, which selected Martin as one of the World's 100 Most Influential People of 2012.

During late December 2011, the Reddit community turned its sights on opposing the election campaigns of candidates for Congress who supported SOPA. Paul Ryan, who was up for reelection and who also would become Mitt Romney's VP pick in 2012, was one of the first targets, in what was called "Operation Pull Ryan." But it turned out that Ryan hadn't even taken a position on SOPA at the time.

Soon after the anti-Ryan campaign started, Ryan wisely announced his opposition to SOPA. In a January 9, 2012 statement, Ryan explained: "The internet is one of the most magnificent expressions of freedom and free enterprise in history. It should stay that way. While H.R. 3261, the Stop Online Piracy Act, attempts to address a legitimate problem, I believe it creates the precedent and possibility for undue regulation, censorship and legal abuse. I do not support H.R. 3261 in its current form and will oppose the legislation should it come before the full House." In a sudden turn of events, Ryan joined the "free Internet" camp.

The stop-SOPA forces were working fast and furious against corporations and Congress members that supported the legislation. Redditors especially were taking no prisoners in their stop-SOPA campaign. By the end of 2011, the sprawling grassroots opposition had gained the upper hand.

*　　*　　*

For much of the SOPA debate, the Obama White House remained noticeably silent. Too silent, in the view of critics. The Obama Administration had been both pro-IP enforcement and pro-Internet companies, with big supporters from both Hollywood and Silicon Valley. Picking sides in the debate would not be easy.

David Sohn of the Center for Democracy & Technology (CDT) saw an opening. CDT had been trying to reach out to the White House to raise CDT's concerns about SOPA. In December 2011, CDT was finally successful in getting a meeting with Howard Schmidt, the Cyber-Security Coordinator for the White House. Schmidt had years of experience in cybersecurity, including stints at eBay, Microsoft, and the Information Security Forum. Sohn helped to organize a meeting for several of the Internet experts who wrote the influential May 2011 white paper to present their concerns about DNS blocking to Schmidt.

The meeting was in early December 2011 at the White House. Things got off to an inauspicious start when one of the Internet engineers, Steve Crocker, set off alarms of the radiation detector at security for the White House. Crocker just had a nuclear medical test that morning, so he still was a little bit radioactive. Good thing Crocker brought a doctor's note for explanation.

The meeting convened in the Situation Room in the basement of the West Wing of the White House, where the President gets intelligence briefings during crises or military operations. The main conference room is perhaps best known today as the location of the now iconic photograph of the meeting of President Obama and his advisers, including a concerned Secretary of State Hillary Clinton with a hand over her mouth, during the successful operation to kill Osama bin Laden. It seemed fitting to discuss SOPA's cyber-security issues in the part of the White House where the President considered national security operations.

The Internet engineers gave their presentation outlining the risk to cybersecurity posed by SOPA. The experts explained how DNS blocking was incompatible with the more secure DNSSEC protocol being developed to reduce cybersecurity threats. Indeed, DNS blocking would thwart the whole idea of establishing a secure system by which each domain name has an authenticated digital signature to verify it as the true owner of the domain. DNS blocking would create, in effect, unverified domains that DNSSEC servers would treat as suspicious. The group of Internet engineers had made similar presentations to Darrell Issa and to staffers of other members of Congress during the summer of 2011. Crocker had come away from those previous meetings with the feeling that the cybersecurity issues they had raised would not be enough to stop SOPA in Congress. There was simply too much politics backing the bill. Crocker hoped that the Obama Administration would be more open to the engineers' analysis.

At the White House meeting, Schmidt and Victoria Espinel, the IP Enforcement Coordinator, mainly listened. If they had a view on SOPA, they didn't tip their hand.

The meeting lasted over an hour and seemed to go well, but

Sohn, Crocker, and the others had no idea which way the White House was leaning. Crocker sensed that the White House was still conflicted, unable to choose sides between Hollywood and Silicon Valley, both of which had provided Obama with a lot of support during his 2008 election campaign. Espinel's office was set up specifically to increase IP enforcement, so it was hard to believe that she didn't support SOPA in some respects.

But if any president could understand why so many people were up in arms about SOPA, President Obama would be it. Obama's election campaign in 2008 had utilized social media on Facebook, YouTube, and Twitter, transforming the way in which presidential campaigns are waged. Obama believed in the power of the Internet to have greater transparency in government. To that end, the White House had set up a way for anyone—under "We the People"—to file an online petition to the Obama Administration. If the petition received 25,000 signatures in 30 days, the White House promised to respond.

Two people, sure enough, petitioned the White House about SOPA. Ryan Bertsche, a college student from the University of Wisconsin-Milwaukee who went by the Reddit username Sevsquad, submitted the first petition back on Halloween 2011, coincidentally the same day Fight for the Future began thinking about a possible day of protest against SOPA. Though Bertsche hadn't been interested in getting involved in national politics before, what he heard about SOPA was alarming. So alarming that the college student, a sophomore, decided to get involved for the first time—and take his concerns "straight to the top," as he put it, meaning to the President.

"This Bill would . . . essentially allow A Great Firewall of America and would be a shameful desecration of free speech and any sort of reasonable copyright law. . . . Essentially it's a censorship law that would end the internet as we know it in America," Bertsche wrote in his petition.[35] A history major, Bertsche didn't realize at the time that he would soon be making history. Bertsche posted a link to the petition on Reddit, which had over 28 million unique visitors per month. Within a day, the petition had over

8,000 signatures. By 17 days, it secured over 30,000, more than enough to ensure that the White House would have to respond. Eventually, the petition garnered over 52,000 signatures.

Bertsche was floored when his friend told him the news. "It was rather surreal; never had anything I put together been considered by anyone with even a hundredth of the importance of the President. I felt like I had skipped several hundred steps on the road of political activism. I mean, up until that point I could barely be bothered to vote, let alone be active in any sort of political group, and suddenly a petition of mine was going to be considered by the President of the United States? It was an excitement that lasted several days, and really sparked my current interest in the political world."

If that were not enough, on December 18, 2011, another Reddit user named EquanimousMind posted another petition, specifically asking President Obama to "VETO the SOPA bill and any other future bills that threaten to diminish the free flow of information." The petition included a quote from President Obama saying, "the more freely information flows; the stronger that society becomes," with a link to the source.[36]

The petition then added:

By allowing free conversation it is so easy to drop a link, http://i.imgur.com/TD4Kq.jpg

It would be ridiculous for an ISP to block the entire whitehouse.gov domain on court order because a single user posted a link. It is difficult for any web administrator to know which links to copyrighted material are done with permission. This will kill the free flow of information and conversation on the internet.

SOPA is too blunt. Please veto.

The petition was trying to be clever. The link was to a webpage that contained a copyrighted cartoon of a person and alien behind bars. The use of the copyrighted cartoon was purportedly an act of copyright infringement. Should the White House be held responsible for that link to infringing material on the Internet posted by a third party? If the logic of SOPA were extended to the White House, it might be on the hook.

House Judiciary Committee Chairman Smith, co-sponsor of SOPA, issued an email response to the petition: "This petition is irrelevant because it does not apply to the Stop Online Piracy Act. Contrary to what the petition says, the Stop Online Piracy Act specifically targets foreign criminals that steal America's products and profits. This bill applies to foreign illegal websites, not lawful domestic sites like whitehouse.gov. And it requires a court order before any action is taken, not just a claim by an individual as some critics wrongly assert."[37]

Smith noted confidently to reporters the week before that he expected the president to sign the bill when passed by Congress.[38]

By this point, though, the SOPA controversy was boiling over.

EquanimousMind linked to the "veto SOPA" petition on Reddit. Within only two days, the petition garnered the necessary 25,000 signatures. Eventually, it would receive over 51,000 signatures. The two petitions against SOPA elicited over 100,000 signatures in record time.

The White House prepared its response within a month. The responsibility fell to Espinel, Schmidt, and Aneesh Chopra, the U.S. Chief Technology Officer.

On January 14, 2012, the three officials released the White House's response on its website, only a day after six key Republican Senators, including Chuck Grassley and Orrin Hatch, asked the Majority Leader Harry Reid to delay the vote on PIPA until the Senate could have more time to study the various objections raised by interested parties. The Republican Senators noted that they had heard from "a large number of constituents and other stakeholders with vocal concerns about possible unintended consequences of the proposed legislation, including breaches in cybersecurity, damaging the integrity of the Internet, costly and burdensome litigation, and dilution of First Amendment rights."[39] With six Republicans backpedaling away from PIPA, Reid probably lacked the 60 votes necessary for cloture to get a vote on the bill as scheduled for January 24, 2012.

The White House response was another huge victory for the opposition to SOPA, especially following on the heels of the six Republican Senators' letter. The White House did not support SOPA, at least not as drafted. And it raised several major concerns that echoed some of the sentiments of the opposition to SOPA.

"While we believe that online piracy by foreign websites is a serious problem that requires a serious legislative response, we will not support legislation that reduces freedom of expression, increases cybersecurity risk, or undermines the dynamic, innovative global Internet."[40] Then, in bold type, the White House indicated: **"Any effort to combat online piracy must guard against the risk of online censorship of lawful activity and must not inhibit innovation by our dynamic businesses large and small."**

The White House explained: "Across the globe, the openness of the Internet is increasingly central to innovation in business, government, and society and it must be protected." To that end, the White House emphasized the need for narrowly-tailored anti-piracy laws against foreign sites, with adequate due process. The White House further warned against tampering with the DNS and "creating new cybersecurity risks or disrupting the underlying architecture of the Internet." SOPA could do exactly that: "Our analysis of the DNS filtering provisions in some proposed legislation suggests that they pose a real risk to cybersecurity and yet leave contraband goods and services accessible online."

The White House concluded by calling for Congress, stakeholders, and the public to come together "to develop new legal tools to protect global intellectual property rights without jeopardizing the openness of the Internet."

Although the White House response, which was released early Saturday, received little media attention that day, the response was nothing short of extraordinary. It validated the SOPA opposition's concerns of Internet censorship, lack of due process, and cybersecurity risks. The Administration also recognized the need to protect the "openness of the Internet," even when attempting to protect intellectual property from piracy. The White House would not support any bill that threatened the openness of the Internet or risked online censorship of lawful expression.

When Ryan Bertsche read the White House response to his petition, he was beside himself. Ecstatic! He immediately called his friends to share the unbelievable news. When he later had time to reflect upon that moment, Bertsche described how special it was: "I couldn't help but think that I helped [to stop SOPA] in a way as well, no matter how small, which is probably one of the most satisfying feelings I have ever felt."

The White House response to the stop-SOPA petition left the bill in serious doubt. Even if SOPA passed Congress, it now seemed very likely that President Obama would veto it.

The President never got that opportunity. After the New Year, SOPA would suffer an even bigger mortal blow that left many of its sponsors fleeing for cover.

Chapter 4
Wikipedia Blackout

January 18, 2012 brought together a vast array of powerful forces on the Internet in a perfect storm. The day would be so big, both in scale and importance, that it would later be commemorated with its own name: Internet Freedom Day.

Following the success of American Censorship Day, several groups—Fight for the Future, Reddit, Wikipedia, and others—were deliberating about their own ideas for a second day of protest. SOPA and PIPA were still alive, so an even bigger Internet protest was needed. The House would be back in session on January 17, and the Senate on January 23. The fear was that Majority Leader Reid could still manage to obtain a successful cloture motion to get a vote on PIPA in January. And then PIPA might be a done deal, perhaps prompting the House to go with the less aggressive bill instead of SOPA. Given the new session of Congress, the opposition to SOPA needed to move fast.

Reddit was the first one to pick a date for its protest: Wednesday, January 18, 2012. The date was chosen to coincide with Reddit co-founder Alexis Ohanian's scheduled testimony about SOPA before the House Committee on Oversight and Government Reform. Chairman Issa invited Ohanian, as well as three experts whose writings on cybersecurity were cited during the SOPA markup (Dan Kaminsky, Stewart Baker, and Dr. Leonard Napolitano), to testify about DNS blocking under SOPA and its effect on Internet security.

The January 18, 2012 hearing before the House Oversight Committee with Reddit's co-founder would be postponed, however. Before the day of the hearing, Majority Leader Eric Cantor had assured Issa that the DNS blocking provision would be dropped from SOPA.[1] And the impending Internet protest was about to draw so many participants that the hearing would be unnecessary. Millions of Americans would provide testimony enough to Congress about the harms SOPA posed to the Internet.

Reddit had never before blacked out its site. But, after an all-staff meeting to discuss SOPA, Eric Martin and the rest of the Reddit staff believed that SOPA threatened its very existence, given the onerous duties it would impose on websites like Reddit. As Martin explained, "This wasn't a political decision for Reddit. This was a business decision. If this law passed, we were very worried about being able to run the site."

On January 10, 2012, Reddit explained its reasons for the blackout in a blog post titled "Stopped They Must Be; On This All Depends."

"Many of you stand with us against PIPA/SOPA, but we know support for a blackout isn't unanimous. We're not taking this action lightly. We wouldn't do this if we didn't believe this legislation and the forces behind it were a serious threat to reddit and the Internet as we know it."

Although Reddit didn't attempt to organize other groups to join its upcoming day of protest, others did. Forces from different parts of the Internet—both large and small—converged together for a day of protest. Fight for the Future and other groups that had participated in American Censorship Day decided to go with January 18 as the date of their second day of protest, although some activists worried that January 18 might be the wrong choice given that the Senate wouldn't be back from its holiday recess. Fight for the Future had originally planned a protest for January 23, the day of the Senate's return, but the momentum for January 18 was now too strong for them to wait until a later date.

Unlike Fight for the Future's previous campaigns, this protest lacked a memorable name. Fight for the Future wanted "SOPA

Strike." But the name that stuck was "Internet blackout," or simply "blackout." Enough said.

Holmes understood the organic nature of the movement to stop SOPA. There were so many players now involved. Fight for the Future was just one of them. Holmes, a literature major in college, couldn't help but get the sense he and his group were feeling what he believed the old Russian General Kutuzov symbolized in Tolstoy's *War and Peace*—a recognition of the limited supporting roles that people play in the course of history and the flow of humanity, with no single person able to change the course. Fight for the Future was but a minor figure in the grassroots movement to stop SOPA. If it was any consolation, at least General Kutuzov helped to stop Napoleon's invasion of Russia. Holmes hoped Fight for the Future could do its small part to stop SOPA.

In some respects, the second SOPA protest was easier to plan than the first, even though the second was much larger in scope. The blueprint was already set. American Censorship Day provided the coalition with the template on how to wage a successful online protest.

The key moment for the Internet blackout occurred when two of the biggest web behemoths—one corporate, the other nonprofit—decided to join the protest: Google and Wikipedia. Google ranked first and Wikipedia eighth in web traffic in the United States, with 153.4 million and 62.1 million unique visitors each month, respectively, according to Nielsen.[2] Google's and Wikipedia's participation in the SOPA protest would ensure that millions of people in the United States and around the world would experience the Internet blackout. Having either web giant participate would have sufficed to make the SOPA protest a huge success. Having both assured SOPA's demise.

As the White House finalized its views on SOPA in the second week of January 2012, Wikipedia was nearing its own decision about the bill. The online encyclopedia was one of the most-visited sites in the world. Given its everyday reach to millions of people, Wikipedia could likely move the needle among the American people more than even the White House could.

By January 2012, the discussion at Wikipedia was no longer about whether SOPA was a bad bill—many people at Wikipedia had already reached that conclusion by December 2011, if not earlier. The discussion now was whether Wikipedia should get involved. Wikipedia was a nonprofit whose mission was to provide information and knowledge to the public. Politics was just not something Wikipedia did.

In order for Wikipedia to break its neutrality, the community itself needed to be on board. That meant Wikipedia needed to have buy-in from the thousands of volunteer writers—the so-called Wikipedians—who make Wikipedia the marvel of crowdsourced creation that it is. The volunteers themselves made the key decisions at Wikipedia. They did the work, and they ran the show.

Wikipedia's founder, Jimmy Wales, floated the idea of a SOPA protest back in December 2011, setting up an informal poll on his webpage.[3] The Italian Wikipedia community provided an example back in October of that year, blacking out its site in a day of protest of an Italian law that would require sites to post corrections, within 48 hours, to comments that were allegedly "detrimental" to any person. Wales thought SOPA was worse than the Italian law and asked people to share their own views.

Over 89% of the people who replied to Wales's informal poll supported a blackout.[4]

Discussions about SOPA continued on the "village pump" of Wikipedia, which was akin to a high-tech water cooler where Wikipedians could chat online about issues related to the organization. In a post on the village pump, Fight for the Future had attempted to get Wikipedia involved in American Censorship Day back in November 2011. Sentiments on the village pump had seemed in favor of a protest, but there had not been enough time or enough of a consensus at that point for the Wikipedia community to reach a decision to join the protest.[5] Now, the momentum appeared to be headed toward a decision to join the second day of protest. But the Wikimedia Foundation, the nonprofit that provides the infrastructure and support for the Wiki sites, needed greater clarity from the Wikipedia community on what, if anything, it wanted to do.

On Friday, January 13, 2012, at 9:23 a.m. PT, the Foundation posted a request for comment (RFC) on the Wikipedia site.[6] Most RFCs on Wikipedia take weeks or even months, but given the exigent circumstances, the RFC on SOPA was expedited, lasting only 76 hours.

Philippe Beaudette, Wikimedia's Director of Community Advocacy who served as the Foundation's liaison to the community, prepared the SOPA RFC. It gave Wikipedians the chance to support and comment on a set of possible actions, ranging from no protest at all to a blackout of Wikipedia of some sort, either a "soft" blackout that allowed a user to click through to the Wikipedia site or a "hard" blackout shutting down nearly all access to Wikipedia for one day. The options also allowed people to express their preferences for a U.S.-only blackout or a complete global blackout of Wikipedia.

On Friday, Beaudette appointed three well-respected Wikipedians to serve as "closers" or "administrators" who would interpret the results of the comments from the community. The administrators were diverse and went by the colorful handles: "Nuclear Warfare" (an anonymous U.S. student), "Risker" (Anne Clin, a hospital risk assessment manager from Canada and a member of Wikipedia's arbitration committee), and Billinghurst (Andrew Billinghurst from Australia, an administrator in the Victorian State government).

In order to make a blackout even a possibility, Wikimedia needed to start making preparations right away. General Counsel Geoff Brigham called a late Friday afternoon meeting of Wikimedia staff on January 13, 2012, in one of the sixth-floor conference rooms in its South of Market office in San Francisco. A late Friday afternoon meeting wasn't exactly what people preferred, but they realized that the SOPA discussions among the community had intensified.

At the Friday the 13th meeting, the group began reading the tea leaves from the ongoing comments on Wikipedia. Based on the RFC responses so far and the earlier comments on the village pump, it looked like Wikipedians preferred a soft blackout of some kind, possibly limited to the United States. It was still early, though, so sentiments could shift. Having no protest at all was still an option. But Wikimedia needed to be prepared for every possibility.

Brigham instructed Brandon Harris, the senior designer, to come up with designs for a soft blackout page. With his long hair and appearance of a heavy metal rock star, Harris had become something of an Internet celebrity. Earlier that year, Wikipedia used his photo in its annual appeal for donations. People loved Harris's photo so much they remixed it into other spoof ads. Harris was so popular he even brought in more donations than founder Jimmy Wales did during the campaign. Besides being a minor Internet star, Harris had extensive web design experience, having worked in design and user interface since basically the start of the Web.

At the meeting, Harris floated three themes for the design. One design was a "dragon slayer" design, the most aggressive, in-your-face design. The second was an understated design, a very simple and muted blackout page. And the third was a stately design, one that conveyed the sense that Wikipedia spoke with authority.

People in the room reached a quick consensus in favor of the stately design. Harris had his marching orders.

After the meeting, Harris stopped by the weekly office happy hour to grab a beer. He knew the importance of what he was about to do, and it started weighing on him. When he went home later that evening, he started becoming really scared, even getting the sweats.

"I've never been more scared in my entire life," Harris admitted afterwards. He knew millions of people and news media from around the world would see his web design for the blackout. It would be a historic occasion. He better not screw up.

With no time to spend fretting, Harris got right down to work. The design would be stately, but, in order to fit the importance of the event, the design also had to be memorable—simple, yet symbolic and even iconic. It had to leave an impression.

As Harris put it, "The design had to convey shock and awe."

The design also had to look good in reduced size, 300 pixels wide, in order to be effective when copied on tech blogs, other websites, and TV news reports.

That night, Harris first sketched out a white mockup of a possible protest page. It started out with a large "W" logo with "Wikipedia" on the left side of the page, and a title and a few lines of text in the middle. Harris found it too plain. He added a shadow effect to the "W" and "Wikipedia," in order to add interest to the design. Harris liked the shadow effect, a cool technique he had perfected in Photoshop, which made the shadow slightly fuzzier at the edges—like a true shadow.

Harris then made a darker version of the same mockup design. He used black as the background, but with varying gradients of black. That allowed him to place the logo "W" prominently on the top left portion of the blacked-out page, with the letter casting an ominous black shadow on the page. The lettering of the title and text was in white. By using shades of gray and black, Harris was able to represent SOPA and PIPA symbolically. The gradient of darkening black depicted the "encroaching darkness" of SOPA and PIPA. By contrast, the "W" and "Wikipedia" were aligned with brightness and the light, representing openness and the forces of good.

The black design for the web page Harris created was, in a word, beautiful. And it was a stark contrast from the normally white pages of Wikipedia.

Remarkably, Harris finished the work in a couple of hours. He sent the two mockups of his designs to Jay Walsh, Head of Communications, for approval. Walsh liked the designs, but made some tweaks to the text. After a few revisions, Walsh said, "This is good to go."

By 11:30 p.m., Harris posted both the black and the white designs on Wikipedia to get comments from the community. Then, after a long day, he went to bed, exhausted.

By the next morning, the Wikipedia community's choice of design was clear: the black version was the winner by a landslide.

Harris spent the weekend coding the design in HTML and CSS, but eventually handed it off to another staff member, Neil Kandalgaonkar, who was a coding whiz. Harris also delegated to Ryan Kaldari, one of Wikimedia's engineers, the unenviable task of creating a directory of contact information for members of Congress. Some nonprofits had volunteered their own directories for Wikipedia to link to, but Harris knew that Wikipedia's massive traffic would crash their servers. So Wikipedia had to build a directory from scratch. The Wikipedia blackout page for U.S. viewers would contain a single call to action in the center of the page—a white box in which the reader could insert a zip code to look up his or her Congress member on a directory created by Wikipedia.

Monday, January 16, 2012 was Martin Luther King, Jr. Day, a holiday in San Francisco. But Wikimedia summoned its staff to the sixth-floor boardroom for an "all hands on deck" emergency meeting. The room became known as the SOPA War Room. Armed with their laptops, people were gearing up for battle.

Early afternoon, the panel of three administrators concluded its review. Over the four days of the RFC, more than 1,800 Wikipedians posted their comments—the largest RFC discussion among Wikipedians ever. Risker instant-messaged the results to Beaudette: *hard blackout, worldwide.*

The message gave Beaudette goose bumps. He announced the result to Brigham and the rest of the small, core SOPA team as they were preparing to address the entire staff. This is pretty awe-inspiring, Beaudette thought to himself, as he announced the verdict to the small team. People in the room didn't say much. They now knew what their task was.

A global blackout of the English-language Wikipedia received the strongest support (55%) in the 1,800-plus comments, with the "overwhelming majority" supporting some form of protest. The Wikipedia community concluded, "[B]oth of these bills, if passed, would be devastating to the free and open web."[7] Two frequently cited objections to SOPA were that it undermined the Digital Millennium Copyright Act (DMCA) safe harbors under which Wikipedia operated, and that it created national barriers on the Internet by blacklisting foreign domain names. Many people viewed SOPA as a direct threat to Wikipedia, and the protest as a fight for the survival of the project. So the die was cast: Wikipedia would publicly oppose the bills by blacking out *all* English-language web pages of Wikipedia around the world.

The historic decision marked the first time the online encyclopedia had ever decided to stake out a political protest through a global blackout of Wikipedia. On behalf of the Wikipedia community, the three administrators requested the Foundation "to allocate resources and assist the community in blacking out the project globally for 24 hours starting at 5:00 UTC on January 18, 2012."

At the offices of Wikimedia, the Foundation went into high gear.

In the SOPA War Room, Wikimedia Foundation's Executive Director Sue Gardner informed the rest of staff of the results of the Wikipedia RFC on SOPA: Wikipedia would have a global blackout that locked down all of its English-language pages.

Wow.

The news was a bit of a surprise. On Friday, they were expecting a soft blackout limited to the United States. But it turned out the community wanted more. The dramatic shift from Friday's early comments to the RFC stemmed from the later participation of many non-U.S.-based Wikipedians who expressed their desire to have the blackout extend to their countries as well. They, too, wanted to be a part of the blackout. The blackout would be hard, not soft, and global in scale. Given the amount of traffic Wikipedia commanded, everyone in the room understood what they were doing would be BIG.

Students and even adults who regularly depend on Wikipedia for information couldn't rely on Wikipedia for an entire day.

Through a tweet, Wales aptly warned students: "Do your homework early."[8]

*   *   *

Initially, Gardner had some reservations about the global blackout. How could she not? She understood Wikipedia's important responsibility in the dissemination of knowledge through its online encyclopedia to millions of people around the world. And she knew that if Wikipedia took a political stance, readers might question the objectivity of Wikipedia's numerous articles. Blacking out Wikipedia in political protest should therefore be reserved for the most exceptional of circumstances. But SOPA was such a circumstance, a serious threat to the free and open Internet. Gardner was entirely on board with the Wikipedia community's decision. Now she needed to make it happen.

In the War Room, responsibilities were assigned. The entire staff was focused and charged. Harris oversaw the design and execution of the technical side of the blackout with his team. He wasn't expecting the "hard" blackout of the site, so the team needed to reconfigure the landing page to lock down the site.

Brigham and Walsh led the team to draft the text and content of the blackout pages—a painstaking process that consumed considerable time. But it was incredibly important to everyone to get the messaging right.

Gardner, who was laboring through the day fighting a bad cold, oversaw the entire process. A preacher's daughter from Port Hope, a small town in Ontario, Canada, she was a journalist by training who had worked at the Canadian Broadcasting Corporation. After joining Wikimedia, Gardner became an even stauncher believer in the power of the Internet—which she described as "one of the wonders of our lifetime"—as a conduit of free speech and the sharing of knowledge.

On that MLK Day, Gardner wrote a blog post explaining Wikipedia's decision to protest SOPA with a global blackout of its site. She described how the community reached the decision and why Wikipedia's departure from its usual position of neutrality was necessary. Gardner felt a responsibility to make Wikipedia's decision transparent to everyone, and to explain to the public why Wikipedia was taking a stand against SOPA.

"My hope is that when Wikipedia shuts down on January 18, people will understand that we're doing it for our readers. We support everyone's right to freedom of thought and freedom of expression. We think everyone should have access to educational material on a wide range of subjects, even if they can't pay for it. We believe in a free and open Internet where information can be shared without impediment. We believe that new proposed laws like SOPA—and PIPA, and other similar laws under discussion inside and outside the United States—don't advance the interests of the general public."[9]

Beaudette created a banner announcing the upcoming blackout on Wikipedia. In the banner, he provided a link to Gardner's blog post. The traffic from Wikipedia was so heavy, it initially crashed Wikimedia's blog servers. Gardner's post generated more than 13,000 comments, the most ever for any Wikimedia post. Most of the comments supported the decision. All showed the high level of engagement with SOPA among Wikipedians. It was off the charts.

Soon after Wikipedia's announcement of the upcoming blackout, Wikimedia was inundated with media calls. The story was already big. Walsh, who had spent many years in communications, had never received as many press calls in his life.

Once given their assignments in the War Room, the staff plunged into their work. A team of volunteers helped out, along with the community of Wikipedians around the world. The blackout of Wikipedia would happen in less than 48 hours, so there was no time to waste. It would take a super-human effort to make Wikipedia go black on January 18.

Gardner, Brigham, Jay Walsh, Board member Kat Walsh, and staff attorney Michelle Paulson worked on numerous drafts of the text to add to the blackout page. Whatever they said, it had to be short. But it also had to convey the right tone and message. Wikipedia wasn't an advocacy group—and didn't want to become one. The message had to explain the reason for the blackout and maintain Wikipedia's credibility.

The group worked on the text in Google Docs, which allowed them to collaborate on the wording at the same time. Multiple versions of the text were vetted not only in the War Room, but online with other Wikipedians around the world. One benefit of having a global operation is having someone in the operation awake at every moment.

The group worked on revisions of the text all the way up to the final minute before the blackout launched. On the day before the blackout, the text went through 50 different revisions. Never before had so many people at Wikipedia spent so much time on so few words. Only 60 words made the final version of the blackout page. That's it.

The group also worked on the text of the SOPA "learn more" fact page where Wikipedia would provide relevant information about SOPA to readers. The SOPA fact page was styled similar to a FAQ page, and had thirteen questions with answers about SOPA and the reason for the blackout.[10]

Meanwhile, Kaldari and his team worked nonstop on the congressional directory. Kaldari had no experience in creating a directory, but, from his days in working on Wikipedia fundraising campaigns, he was always up for a challenge involving tight deadlines, even all-nighters. Kaldari brought in the help of two other Wikimedia software engineers, Katie Horn from fundraising and Arthur Richards from mobile development.

Building the congressional directory was an absolute bear. Things got so harried, the team decided to leave the War Room and bunker down in some cubicles to focus entirely on the directory—with no distractions.

The main problem was that there was no free, up-to-date database of contact information for the 535 members of Congress. Turnover happens every two years in the House, so databases of congressional contact information can become obsolete really fast. Given the time and costs of creating a directory based on full addresses, Kaldari and his team decided to go with a second-best solution of using only 5-digit zip codes for Wikipedia's "look up" directory.

That solution created another problem: the 50,000 zip codes in the United States did not correlate perfectly with congressional districts, which meant that Wikipedia's "look up" feature couldn't always provide a person with the single representative for her district. Instead, where several districts overlapped with a zip code, the directory would provide all the representatives for the particular zip code and then let the user hopefully identify—or guess—the right one. Kaldari and the Wikimedia team debated whether to have the database incorporate 9-digit zip codes to get a more targeted search by district, but they decided to stick with 5-digit zip codes out of necessity: most people don't know their 9-digit zip codes. The solution was not ideal, but it was the best they could do in two days.

To create the database, Kaldari started with the Sunlight Foundation's open-source directory of Congress, but then had to verify and update the listings and contact information manually by comparing the data with other sources like Govtrack.us. If Kaldari had a couple weeks, that task would have been easy. But with less than two days, he was nervous. It did not seem humanly possible.

To add to their task, the team decided to add the Twitter handles of the Congress members, in addition to phone numbers and website information, so that people could contact their legislators in a variety of ways, including by tweeting.

Another problem in creating the directory was ensuring that it would scale. Millions of Wikipedia users would likely look up their Congress members at the same time, so Kaldari knew they had to have a caching or duplicate storage system in place to accommodate the traffic to Wikipedia's directory.

Kaldari's team plowed through the night and next day, trying to get the directory of 535 members of Congress up and running. As the blackout neared, Kaldari became even more nervous they wouldn't finish in time. Things were frantic. In the last few hours, Kaldari and his team worked furiously to get the data cleaned up and the bugs out of the software. The team enlisted Ariel Glenn, a Wikimedia software developer from Greece, to help out. Unfortunately, there was too much information to look up and update in the directory, so the team decided they would have to keep on updating the information even during the blackout after it went live. But Kaldari would be happy—and relieved—to get the "look up" directory at least operational by the witching hour. Not perfect, but good enough.

Most of the staff and volunteers in San Francisco worked around the clock, in different shifts, so people could alternate getting a few hours of sleep. Gardner herself stayed in the War Room until 4 a.m. PT, when Brigham came back to the office after his short rest. One of them was always around to oversee the planning. There was so much work, and so little time, but the entire staff poured their energies into getting it all done. They all understood the historic nature of what they were about to do. A staff member took photos of the planning in the War Room on the day before the blackout and posted them on the Wikimedia Commons to memorialize the event.[11]

People were excited to be a part of the SOPA protest because they believed the bill was a threat to the free and open Internet. Fighting to protect the Internet was a cause they all shared. But they also had mixed feelings about shutting down Wikipedia, even for just a day. Denying people access to the knowledge of Wikipedia ran counter to their free-knowledge convictions, so they all felt a profound sense of responsibility for what they were about to do. Millions of people would be affected. It was sobering. No one took the blackout lightly.

As Harris later reflected, "For a lot of us, keeping the site up is an emotional thing, our mission. So to actively go against our mission for a bit was kind of complicated. It was a very confusing position to be in, even though we agreed with the blackout."

A minute before the blackout, Richards finally finished the computer scripts for the "lookup" database cache. Without the cache, the heavy traffic from the blackout would likely have crashed the servers. With only seconds to spare, Richards texted Kaldari: *cache warm up scripts JUST finished :).*

At 9 p.m. PT on January 17, 2012, which was midnight January 18 on the East coast, the blackout of Wikipedia went live. Kaldari and Ryan Lane, an operations guy, had the weighty responsibility of flipping the switch to make Wikipedia go black. Kaldari turned on the central notice to make the blackout overlay go live, while Lane turned off the editing function to all Wikipedia pages. The deed was done.

The screen in the War Room projected the striking image of Wikipedia's website all blacked out.[12] The site read:

"Imagine a World Without Free Knowledge."

The captivating title had been suggested by Sarah Stierch, a Wikimedia Foundation Community Fellow in DC who had just started at Wikimedia that week. Stierch came up with the line in response to a few commenters on an internal Wikipedia listserv who were apathetic about the whole SOPA debate. Stierch's comment drew great buzz on the listserv, which caught the attention of the Wikimedia staff.

The line was a clever riff on Jimmy Wales's mission statement for Wikipedia: "Imagine a world in which every single person on the planet is given free access to the sum of all human knowledge."

Stierch flipped the idea into imagining a world *without* free knowledge under SOPA. In six short words, the statement conveyed the reason why Wikipedia was taking this stand. Gardner, Walsh, and the others knew they had their title. Only six hours before the blackout, Kaldari instant-messaged Stierch to tell her they would run her comment as the title of the blackout page. Stierch was alone in her DC apartment in Logan Circle when she received the news. She was so overwhelmed she was brought to tears.

The blackout page next explained the reason for Wikipedia's decision: "For over a decade, we have spent millions of hours building the largest encyclopedia in human history. Right now, the U.S. Congress is considering legislation that could fatally damage the free and open Internet. For 24 hours, to raise awareness, we are blacking out Wikipedia. Learn more."

The sleep-deprived staff members rejoiced. Gardner, Harris, Paulson, Beaudette, and communications manager Matthew Roth stood and raised their arms in victory, while the rest of the staff cheered in jubilation. A staffer captured the historic moment on video and posted it on the Wikimedia Commons.[13] Their round-the-clock preparations had finally come to fruition. Seeing Wikipedia all blacked out was a sight to behold.

To celebrate, people in the War Room toasted the occasion with beers and a chocolate cake with "SOPA" crossed out in white icing. Everyone was exhausted, working on only a few hours of sleep, so the mood in the room was borderline giddy.

Fittingly, Beaudette and Gayle Karen Young, the newly hired Chief Talent and Culture Officer, cranked up a song to commemorate the occasion: "We're Not Gonna Take It."

Dee Snider would be proud. Though now a bit campy, the rebellious metal song by the popular '80s band Twisted Sister captured what they were feeling.

> *We're not gonna take it. No, we ain't gonna take it. . . .*
> *This is our life, this is our song. We'll fight the powers that be. Just don't pick our destiny 'cause you don't know us. . . .*
> *We're right. We're free. We'll fight. You'll see!*
> *Oh, we're not gonna take it anymore.*

Wikipedia had taken the fight right to Congress. SOPA didn't stand a chance.

*   *   *

On January 17, 2012, a day before the blackout, Google announced its own historic decision to join the protest: "We oppose these bills because there are smart, targeted ways to shut down foreign rogue Web sites without asking American companies to censor the Internet."[14]

The move had been foreshadowed by Google Executive Chairman Eric Schmidt's denunciation of SOPA's DNS blocking requirement as censorship back in November 2011.[15] Google didn't go as far as blacking out its entire site, but instead opted for a blackout of its well-known "Google" logo on its home page, similar to what Mozilla did on American Censorship Day. Google would remain up and running, allowing people to conduct searches.[16] Google would also add an online petition asking its users to tell their Congress members to stop SOPA/PIPA. The momentous decision marked the first time Google ever used its home page for a protest of any kind or for a political appeal to its millions of users.

When asked about the impending Internet blackout and

protest of SOPA, Representative Smith dismissed the blackout as a "publicity stunt" and suggested that Wikipedia and the opponents of SOPA were "spreading misinformation" about the bill.[17] Smith was determined to proceed forward with the bill, although he announced that he would withdraw the controversial DNS-blocking provision after the White House and many others opposed it. Senator Leahy also dropped DNS blocking from PIPA in the Senate, albeit begrudgingly while noting its importance for law enforcement to combat piracy. The concession from the bills' sponsors would be too little, too late.

The night before the Internet blackout, the folks at Fight for the Future readied their preparation, making sure their websites were updated with the latest news of the protest and information about SOPA. The group built a new website, SOPAstrike.com, for the day of protest, adding to their existing arsenal of websites. Those sites would receive over 12 million unique visitors on the day of the protest, setting an all-time record for Fight for the Future.

When midnight struck on January 18, the group noticed that Google had already blacked out its logo on its home page, with a link stating: "Tell Congress: Please don't censor the web!" The link directed people to an online petition to Congress to reject SOPA/PIPA.

Even though Holmes, Tiffiniy, Nick, and Dean knew about Google's upcoming involvement in the SOPA blackout, to see the iconic Google logo all blacked out blew them away.

The group convened an after-midnight conference call to share their glee.

During the call, they could hardly contain themselves—screaming over the phone with excitement—while discussing the impending blackout. It was unbelievable.

As Holmes later reflected about the historic moment, "This bill was something millions of lobbying dollars and hundreds of lobbyists had worked on over the past two or three years. But the thing about to happen tomorrow was their worst nightmare, literally the worst thing they could possibly imagine happening to their work. They could have never seen it coming. Because nothing like that had ever happened before."

All of Fight for the Future's hard work, along with the hard work of many others who had joined the opposition to SOPA over the past four months, had made a difference. Things were about to go down, in a big way.

As Holmes and the others put it during their gleeful call, enjoying a rare moment of schadenfreude, there was a major "shitstorm" on SOPA about to happen.

And they were right. A shitstorm it was.

*   *   *

The January 18th Internet blackout was the biggest online protest ever. Over 115,000 websites participated in the blackout, including Google, Wikipedia, Craigslist, Reddit, Tumblr, and Wordpress.[18] Facebook, the second most-visited site in the United States, did not use its social network in the protest, but its CEO Mark Zuckerberg issued a statement against SOPA and PIPA on his Facebook page, which had nearly 16 million followers.[19]

Wikipedia reported that 162 million people experienced the blackout trying to access Wikipedia that day. The "look up" feature turned out to be one of the most successful features of the entire blackout. Eight million people looked up their Congress members from the directory created by Wikipedia.[20] Websites of various senators were taken down because the servers could not handle all the traffic to the sites.[21]

Sue Gardner got great satisfaction from all of the positive feedback she received from people, including a proud father who informed her that his 12-year-old daughter had just written her first letter to Congress, thanks to Wikipedia's protest.

Back at Reddit, Erik Martin knew the blackout had really succeeded when his sister, an art teacher at a Brooklyn middle school, called him to let him know that her grade school students all wanted to know why Google was blacked out that day. That's when she started discussing SOPA—and copyright law—with her adolescent students.

The popular, free online Khan Academy, started by Salman Khan as a way to tutor his cousin in math long-distance through YouTube, even devoted an entire American Civics lesson on SOPA to educate its 6 million monthly "students" about the bill and its threats to speech.[22] In less than a year, the video received over 1.4 million views.[23]

Google secured over 7 million signatures to its online petition asking Congress to reject SOPA and PIPA, and several million more were collected by other sites.[24] Four million emails were sent to Congress through EFF's, Fight for the Future's, and Demand Progress's websites.[25] Senator Ben Cardin of Maryland said his office received over 2,000 emails on SOPA/PIPA on that day alone, and over 3,000 emails total. Senator Herb Kohl, a sponsor of PIPA, received over 440 calls related to PIPA/SOPA that day.[26]

Public Knowledge's Ernesto Falcon was on the Hill visiting some staffers, and he saw the same scene in every office he visited: the receptionists were fielding calls non-stop about SOPA. When Falcon got a chance to talk to some of the staffers, they all said the same thing: "Everyone hates this bill." Even that was an understatement.

SOPA overtook social media as well. On January 18, over 3 million tweets mentioned "SOPA," "PIPA," "sopastrike," "blackout-SOPA," or "stopSOPA."[27] In the SOPA War Room, the Wikimedia staff projected a Twitter feed on the screen, with all the tweets mentioning SOPA. Once the blackout started, the tweets of SOPA went berserk. Tweets raced through the SOPA feed like a slot machine gone out of control. It was dizzying.

Wikipedia's blackout sparked an uprising even among Hollywood celebrities.

Ashton Kutcher tweeted to his 12 million-plus followers: "Please don't ignore what's happening here. IMPORTANT MOMENT IN HISTORY! #StopSOPA http://en.wikipedia. org/wiki/Main_Page."[28] Kutcher's comment was then retweeted by others over 4,000 times. Kutcher, who also was a savvy investor in Internet startups, was not new to the SOPA debate. He had written a blog post criticizing SOPA back in December 2011, warning: "It is a disastrous precedent to have Congress legislate Internet DNS control."[29] Kutcher tweeted his blog post, with the following message: "SOPA is the problem and not the solution," which then received a welcoming tweet from Representative Issa.[30]

Kim Kardashian tweeted a similar message: "We must stop SOPA/PIPA to keep the web open & free. Click here http://en.wikipedia.org/wiki/Main_Page to learn more about how u can help fight this legislation." Her tweet, which went out to her 15 million followers, was retweeted over 2,500 times.[31] Back at EFF, Trevor Timm realized, at that moment, the protest had succeeded: even Kim Kardashian knew about and opposed SOPA.

With two little tweets by Kutcher and Kardashian, the call to protest SOPA likely reached more than 25 million people. Quite a feat. Kutcher and Kardashian were just minor figures, though, in a massive protest involving millions of people. The Center for Democracy & Technology kept, on its website, a running list of companies, experts, and individuals from a range of areas and industries that had expressed concern with or opposition to SOPA.[32] The list kept growing and generated tremendous traffic to its site.

The SOPA protest even went low tech. Fight for the Future helped organize town hall meetings in various states to allow people to air their concerns about SOPA. People took to the streets in New York City, San Francisco, Seattle, and DC to protest SOPA with traditional demonstrations and picketing.

A thousand people protested outside the NYC offices of Senators Charles Schumer and Kirsten Gillibrand, both co-sponsors of PIPA.[33] The New York Tech Meetup, a nonprofit with over 20,000 members from the tech industry in New York, helped organize the demonstrations. And with his testimony before the House Oversight Committee postponed, Reddit co-founder Alexis Ohanian was able to make the NYC protest. "This is an issue that has become much bigger than saving the Internet now," Ohanian declared. The young entrepreneur, who was named after boxing champion Alexis Arguello, was determined to knock out SOPA. "This is a fight to save democracy."

In San Francisco, former rap star MC Hammer, who was a part

of a new search engine startup, spoke out against SOPA. Standing among a motley crew of venture capitalists, startup founders, and tech people outside the Civic Center, Hammer warned, "We don't want people who spend their days legislating to try and control creativity. We don't want them to stifle creativity. . . .

"On the surface, they say it's to protect rights and content. That may be the surface. But underneath it, as you drill down, you see all of these other causes that would put a tremendous burden on service providers and whole lot of other people, and give the government the ability to shut down sites without due process. This is just barbaric in its very nature."[34]

For SOPA, the January 18th blackout was Hammer time.

In the aftermath, support and enthusiasm for SOPA and PIPA began to evaporate in Congress. The bills had become toxic.

In the Senate, 19 senators, including 10 who had co-sponsored the bill, expressed their opposition to PIPA after the blackout, joining Senator Wyden and three other senators who had already opposed the bill.[35] The overwhelming majority of the newly-announced opposition (15 Senators) were Republicans.

The Republican tilt to the growing PIPA opposition might have been due to the compatibility between conservative, libertarian principles and the "free Internet" culture. Both camps were skeptical of government regulation of the Internet. The libertarian Heritage Foundation came out strongly against SOPA.[36] As an extra incentive for the Republican senators, the conservative blog RedState made opposition to SOPA a benchmark or expectation for any Republican candidate seeking office or reelection in order to earn conservatives' support.[37] Validating the truism that politics makes strange bedfellows, conservatives and the liberal-leaning Reddit community were both using SOPA as a litmus test for political candidates.

Supporting SOPA was now political suicide for any conservative candidate for Congress.

As Senator Marco Rubio of Florida—a rising star in the Republican ranks, possible future presidential candidate, and a former co-sponsor of PIPA—conceded on his Facebook page on the day of the protest: "We've heard legitimate concerns about the impact the bill could have on access to the Internet and about a potentially unreasonable expansion of the federal government's power to impact the Internet."[38]

Eight members of the House also withdrew their support of SOPA on January 18.[39] Six were Republicans, and two were Democrats. And the total number of House members who opposed SOPA went from 31 to 122 by the day after the Wikipedia blackout.[40]

The January 18th blackout was so big that it made SOPA an issue for the Republican candidates for President at their debate the next day. Discussion of copyright policy was virtually unheard of at a presidential debate, but not after SOPA.

CNN's John King asked a question sent in by a viewer through Twitter: "'What is your take on SOPA, and how do you believe it affects Americans?' For those who have not been following it, SOPA is the Stop Online Piracy Act, a crackdown on Internet piracy, which clearly is a problem. But its opponents say it's censorship. Full disclosure: Our parent company, Time Warner, says we need a law like this, because some of its products, movies, programming, and the like are being ripped off online—"[41]

Even before King could finish his question, he received a smattering of boos from the Florida audience who appeared to take issue with King's claim that Time Warner needed greater protection from online piracy.

Newt Gingrich was licking his chops, ready with an answer, giving almost a disdainful look to CNN's John King, who had suggested that there were two sides to the issue. "You're asking a conservative about the economic interest of Hollywood?"

The audience erupted in applause.

"I'm weighing it. I'm weighing it. I'm trying to think through all the left-wing people who are so eager to protect [their IP]. And you have virtually everyone who is technologically advanced, including Google, YouTube, and Facebook, and all the folks who say this is going to totally mess up the Internet. And the bill in its current form is written really badly and leads to a range of censorship that is totally unacceptable. Well, I favor freedom."

More applause.

"If the company finds it has genuinely been infringed upon, it has the right to sue. But the idea we are going to preemptively have the government start censoring the Internet on behalf of giant corporations' economic interests strikes me as exactly the wrong thing to do."

The audience was ecstatic. Gingrich hit a home run.

Mitt Romney went up next and was smart to agree with Gingrich, given the audience's raucous reaction. "The law, as written, is far too intrusive, far too expansive, far too threatening to speech and movement of information across the Internet. It would have a potentially depressing impact on one of the fastest-growing industries in America, which is the Internet and all those industries connected to it. I'd say that's a mistake. I'm standing for freedom."[42]

Among conservatives, SOPA had become a threat to freedom itself. Many Republicans were having second thoughts about supporting Hollywood's efforts to clamp down on online piracy at all costs. As Stewart Baker, the prominent Republican lawyer who had warned about SOPA's harm to cybersecurity, later wrote in *The Hollywood Reporter*, "SOPA has pushed a generation of Republicans into choosing sides between Hollywood and the Internet."[43] And, in that choice, Hollywood had no chance.

Regardless of which side in the SOPA debate one stood on, the debate signaled a turning point for copyright legislation in Congress. Free speech—and fears of government censorship of the Internet—became a pivotal issue raised by many Americans to their Congress members and to the President. Too many people, businesses, and Internet experts raised concerns about SOPA for Congress to ignore. Democracy, in other words, worked.

As Reddit's GM Erik Martin reflected about the opposition to SOPA: "It was a fight started by activists. But it was not a fight won by activists. It was won by individuals, by communities, by companies like Reddit, which was never political about anything, taking a stand and saying this would affect me, and by tons of other startups and websites blacking out their sites."

If the SOPA protests proved anything, it showed what the American people think should matter to Congress. And, sometimes, it does.

As Falcon explained, "People can have a huge difference in Congress. But people don't believe that. From working on the Hill myself, very few people actually engage with their members of Congress. Any time that changes, and people do get involved, that's when the lobbying money doesn't matter. If you can convince a politician that a whole bunch of voters are upset about an issue, it doesn't matter how much money is being spent on the other side."

By 48 hours after the Internet blackout, the writing was on the wall. Senate Majority Leader Reid announced he would delay any vote on cloture for PIPA, effectively leaving it in limbo. A few hours later, House Judiciary Committee Chair Smith stated that he would postpone consideration of SOPA in a conciliatory message: "I have heard from the critics, and I take seriously their concerns regarding proposed legislation to address the problem of online piracy. It is clear that we need to revisit the approach on how best to address the problem of foreign thieves that steal and sell American inventions and products."[44]

Senator Leahy, the chief sponsor of PIPA, was not as conciliatory. Leahy lamented, "Somewhere in China today, in Russia today, and in many other countries that do not respect American intellectual property, criminals who do nothing but peddle in counterfeit products and stolen American content are smugly watching."[45]

When Holmes heard the good news of SOPA's defeat while he was in Puerto Rico with his family, he breathed a long sigh of relief. Fight for the Future had contingency plans on what to do if the blackout failed to stop SOPA. The group had been working with Senator Wyden's office to make his upcoming filibuster a spectacle on the Internet. Fortunately, Plan B wasn't needed. Fight for the Future sent out an email that day to the stop-SOPA coalition, thanking everyone for standing up for free speech on the Internet. Afterwards, Holmes headed to the beach with his family for some much needed relaxation, still basking in what Fight for the Future had helped to accomplish.

Back in Western Massachusetts, Tiffiniy was brimming with joy. She, too, felt the importance of what the coalition had just accomplished. "This was a watershed moment in political history. If you think about how much was invested in making sure these bills passed and how much support there was on these bills, the fact that we turned that around in a space of three months, between November, December, and January, that's . . . unbelievable. It shows what people care about. This was a fight for free speech."

Sue Gardner, who averaged only three hours of sleep during each of the previous three nights, shared a congratulatory message with the Wikipedia community on her blog. "Wikipedia's involvement in the fight against SOPA proves this wasn't about powerful interest groups, and it wasn't about money. Wikipedia is operated, and not controlled, by a non-profit—it's got no corporate interests to protect and it doesn't make any money from piracy or copyright infringement. It's written by ordinary people. . . .

"What happened yesterday is that around the world, Internet users found their voice—fighting back against people who wanted to threaten their freedoms."[46]

Completely exhausted, Gardner finally went home the day after the blackout at 4 a.m. for her first good night's sleep that week.

Representative Issa posted a congratulatory message on his website as well: "THIS JUST IN!! YOU GUYS STOPPED PIPA (SOPA's Senate counterpart)! Internet mutiny paired with calls from people across the country certainly must be responsible for Harry Reid's decision to 'postpone Tuesday's vote on the PRO-TECT IP Act.' For now, we can take a breath of relief. But we've still got our eye on both SOPA & PIPA."[47]

Issa knew to strike when the iron was hot. On that day, he formally introduced his alternative OPEN Act in the House, with 17 Democrat and 8 Republican co-sponsors.[48]

On the other side, the mood was quite different. Motion Picture Association of America (MPAA) Chairman and former Senator Christopher Dodd expressed surprise and amazement at the success of the online protests. Many had thought SOPA was a slam dunk in Congress, he conceded. But the protests changed things so dramatically and quickly, garnering incredible support. Likening the SOPA protest to the mass political demonstrations in various Middle Eastern countries in the Arab Spring of 2010 and 2011, Dodd said he couldn't recall an effort that had caused as dramatic a change on legislation in Congress in the past 40 years.[49] Dodd sounded more contrite than he did the day before in his press release, which blasted the blackout as a "stunt" and "abuse of power."[50]

Some sponsors of the bills were even willing to admit mistakes.

Senator Chris Coons, a co-sponsor of the "Bieber bill," conceded that parts of SOPA "overreached . . . [and] really did pose some risk to the Internet."[51] Not only that, but he and the other sponsors of the bills did a poor job in explaining them to the American public.

Coons said he knew they had a problem when one of his young sons woke him to ask a pressing question troubling the boy: Dad, why does Justin Bieber think you should go to jail?

A serious problem, indeed.

Chapter 5
NO to ACTA

The Wikipedia blackout on January 18, 2012 was reported around the world from Australia to Zimbabwe.[1] Even in China, the SOPA story had legs. News outlets in China widely reported the mass protest against SOPA and the public's concerns about Internet censorship by the U.S. government. Sohu.com, a popular Internet portal and one of the Top 10 most trafficked sites in China, quoted the analysis of Chinese blogger Ruan Yifeng, an IT developer who had a PhD in economics.[2] In a blog post titled "Why SOPA Is a Bad Law," Yifeng concluded: "This bill will actually legalize Internet censorship."[3] To underscore the point, the post linked to the Wikipedia entry for "Internet censorship."

China's government—much maligned around the world for its Internet censorship—probably was pleased to see the United States on the receiving end of similar criticisms. Very pleased.

Back in Europe, the timing of the Wikipedia blackout couldn't have been any more inopportune—or opportune, depending on one's position—for the 27 countries of the European Union considering whether to ratify a controversial anti-piracy treaty called ACTA, short for the Anti-Counterfeiting Trade Agreement.

Like SOPA, ACTA was meant to increase enforcement measures against piracy and counterfeiting, only this time by a plurilateral agreement among mainly developed countries including the United States, the European Union (EU), Japan, Australia, New

Zealand, Canada, South Korea, and Singapore. Mexico and Morocco were the only two developing countries involved. ACTA contained a medley of provisions to combat infringement of copyrights and trademarks. But the part that drew the most public reaction was the Internet chapter, which was intended to combat piracy and trade in counterfeit goods on the Internet. Like SOPA, ACTA's Internet chapter sparked fears of Internet censorship.

Much of the controversy over ACTA stemmed from the way in which developed countries negotiated the agreement—in secret. The secrecy roiled people's fears that government trade officials would bargain away people's freedoms—especially on the Internet—to serve Hollywood and large corporate interests in protecting intellectual property. Even if that wasn't necessarily true, the secrecy over ACTA troubled many people who expected greater transparency from their governments, especially in the development of trade policies that would affect millions of people around the world.

The seeds of ACTA started in 2006 during the Bush Administration. But the negotiations intensified in 2009 under President Barack Obama, with United States Trade Representative Ron Kirk leading the U.S. delegation that would eventually secure a final agreement in October 2011 (coincidentally, only a few weeks before SOPA was introduced in Congress). Although Bush and Obama didn't see eye-to-eye on most issues, on ACTA and fighting the war against piracy, they stood united.

The Obama Administration even asserted that ACTA didn't need Congress's approval but could be implemented into U.S. law as a sole executive agreement, adopted unilaterally by the President.

Harvard Law professors Jack Goldsmith, a conservative who served in the Office of Legal Counsel during the Bush Administration, and Larry Lessig, a liberal who supported Obama's election, wrote a scathing *Washington Post* op-ed criticizing the Obama Administration's decision to bypass legislative scrutiny of ACTA.[4] The President's implementation of ACTA without Congress's approval would likely violate the Constitution, in their view. Eventually, the Obama Administration abandoned the sole executive argument and claimed instead that ACTA was simply a measure tacitly authorized ahead of time by Congress in the PRO-IP Act of 2008. Harold Koh, the former Yale Law School Dean and then-Legal Advisor to the State Department, floated the theory in a letter to Senator Ron Wyden, who had challenged the Administration's position and served as a gadfly to ACTA just as he did to SOPA.[5] Koh's theory drew sharp criticism from Wyden, plus fifty law professors including Goldsmith and Lessig.[6] Undaunted, the Obama Administration persisted in its controversial view of ACTA.

The way in which the ACTA negotiations proceeded left a lot to be desired. Starting in May 2008, unofficial draft texts of ACTA appeared on Wikileaks, the controversial site that disseminated leaks of sensitive materials as a form of whistleblowing. Over the next two years, the leaks of ACTA would foment people's fears that governments were devising ways to impose draconian regulations on the Internet, including a "3 strikes" policy on Internet users under which they could lose their Internet access if they were accused of engaging in copyright infringement three times on the Internet. France had a controversial "3 strikes" law known by the agency set up to administer it: HADOPI, or the High Authority for the Protection of Works on the Internet. The Constitutional Council of France ruled, however, that HADOPI violated the freedom of expression by depriving people of the freedom of speech without due process.[7] The French legislature later amended HADOPI to require court review of the allegations of "3 strikes" before a person could lose Internet access. People feared that the ACTA trade negotiators were trying to make countries more like France by exporting its "3 strikes" approach to other countries. A scary thought.

The public backlash that was brewing against ACTA may have helped to convince the negotiating countries to pull back from their original plans. By the time the final text of ACTA came out in May 2011, the negotiators had revised major sections of the Internet chapter of ACTA. "Three strikes" was out of ACTA.

But that didn't end the controversy.

The vague Internet provisions that ended up in the final text of ACTA read like the inkblots of the Rorschach test. People could read into them whatever they wanted. Each of the eight provisions in the Internet chapter focused on combating infringement on the Internet. That much was clear. To some observers, ACTA read more like a directive to police the Internet—to borrow ACTA's own words, taking "effective action against an act of infringement of intellectual property rights which takes place in the digital environment, including expeditious remedies to prevent infringement and remedies which constitute a deterrent to further infringements."[8]

Following on the heels of the Wikipedia blackout on January 18, 2012, the signing of ACTA for the European Union couldn't have been slated for a worse time. Non-governmental organizations (NGOs), public interest groups, activists, and academics had been working for several years to call public attention to ACTA and its dangers, but without much success. The timing of the Wikipedia blackout, however, gave a spark to the ACTA debate. The EU's signing was less than a week away, on January 26, 2012, at a ceremony in Tokyo. Even though SOPA and ACTA were different, and ACTA's Internet chapter was probably not as invasive as the Internet regulations contemplated under SOPA, the stain of SOPA after the Wikipedia blackout spilled over to ACTA.

In the alphabet soup of anti-piracy measures, SOPA and ACTA were considered synonymous. Many in the media and public saw SOPA and ACTA as part and parcel of the same anti-piracy debate—stoking the same fears that ACTA might lead to Internet censorship and restrictions similar to the kind contemplated under SOPA. The perceived connection to SOPA did not bode well for ACTA. By January 2012, SOPA had become a four-letter word. And it would only be time before ACTA would, too.

* * *

Validating the truism that all news is local, the Polish news reports following the Wikipedia blackout framed it in terms of its ramifications for Poland, including the upcoming signing of ACTA the next week. Even though SOPA was a U.S. bill, it was intended to regulate foreign websites suspected of counterfeiting or piracy. So it was relevant to Poland insofar as it could block access in the United States to a Polish website accused of being a foreign rogue site. And the United States' possible interference with the Internet's architecture was an issue that affected all countries, not just Poland.

On January 18, 2012, Polish media interviewed Paweł Zienowicz, a spokesperson for the Polish Wikimedia, about its participation in the blackout. Zienowicz said the Polish Wikimedia would issue a statement in support of the American-based blackout, but did not intend to black out the Polish-language Wikipedia.[9] Some of the Polish NGOs that dealt with Internet policy had tried to persuade the Polish Wikipedia to join the blackout, but Polish Wikipedians were reluctant to join the political debate on the U.S. bill or depart from the site's position of neutrality.

ACTA was a different story. The EU and Poland were directly involved. Zienowicz warned that people might protest the EU's signing of ACTA, which was negotiated in secret, outside of public scrutiny. "The law, which is to have an impact on the lives of all people on Earth, cannot be passed in secret," he told a news reporter.

Zienowicz's warning proved to be prescient. The next day, events would unfold that ignited a popular rebellion that would sweep across Poland.

Igor Ostrowski, the Deputy Minister of the newly created Ministry of Administration and Digitization, hosted a meeting of the "Dialogue Group" on January 19, 2012. The Group was an ad hoc group of businesses, NGOs, and other stakeholders that was formed in 2010 to advise the Polish government on their views related to laws that could affect the Internet. An ill-conceived proposal to require DNS blocking of gambling sites—an idea that eventually was rejected—provided the genesis of the Group.

Attending that day were representatives from businesses and various NGOs in Poland. The NGOs were particularly well-represented and included members from the Internet Society Poland, Modern Poland Foundation, Digital Center Project, Panoptikon, Free and Open Source Software Foundation, and the Helsinki Foundation for Human Rights. The NGOs had raised concerns about ACTA for several years while the negotiations among countries proceeded in secret. Despite the NGOs' concerns, ACTA had remained largely under the radar of the mainstream media and the general public. Until now.

The meeting was held in a conference room at the Prime Minister's Office at 11 a.m., just as the Wikipedia blackout was finishing up in a different time zone back in the United States. Internet policy—and protest—were fresh on everyone's mind.

Ostrowski invited representatives from the Ministry of Culture and Natural Heritage and the Ministry of Economy to the meeting to give a report on ACTA. As a trade agreement, ACTA initially fell within the jurisdiction of the Ministry of Economy, headed by Minister Waldemar Pawlak, who had twice before served as Prime Minister of Poland. Because of the copyright issues in ACTA, the Ministry of Economy transferred the responsibility to the Ministry of Culture, a government office designed to preserve and promote Polish culture, including its authors and artists. Led by Minister Bogdan Zdrojewski, the Ministry of Culture included an Intellectual Property and Media Department that worked on IP laws and enforcement. The Ministry also fielded the requests of the entertainment industry and collecting societies for copyright holders.

The meeting took a dramatic turn—for the worse—when the representative of the Ministry of Economy said that he didn't know what all the discussion was about. Poland was signing ACTA next week. It was too late for discussion.

The NGO reps were stunned. Even speechless.

Based on earlier statements by Prime Minister Donald Tusk's administration, the NGO reps believed the government wouldn't make any final decision on ACTA without holding public consultations and debate.[10] But, apparently, Prime Minister Tusk no longer saw a need for them, at least not with the NGOs or the general public.

Deputy Minister Ostrowski didn't have a say in the decision, despite his background in Internet policy. Ostrowski, an intellectual property lawyer, had worked for several years with the Polish NGO community on Internet issues. Ostrowski's interest in Internet policy was, in a way, therapeutic.

Diagnosed with Stage III colon cancer in 2008, Ostrowski decided, upon his doctor's recommendation, to resign from the demanding position as partner in the Warsaw office of a top New York law firm and, after his medical treatment, to return to work slowly by doing volunteer work.

Starting in 2009, Ostrowski volunteered to serve as a Strategic Advisor to the Prime Minister regarding Internet policy. On the Board of Strategic Advisors, Ostrowski met Alek Tarkowski, a young sociologist with a PhD from the University of Warsaw who was soon becoming a leading figure in Poland's Internet community. Tarkowski was the head of the Polish chapter of Creative Commons, the nonprofit Larry Lessig started to provide alternative forms of mass licensing of copyrighted works in order to promote greater access to culture. Tarkowski and Ostrowski co-founded Poland's Digital Center Project, a think tank focused on developing ways to foster civic, cultural, and social engagement through the Internet. They also co-authored a position paper titled *Poland 2030*, which recommended a long-term strategic approach for Poland's development.[11]

Ostrowski looked concerned about the Ministry of Economy's bombshell.

"This is a big surprise to me," he confessed. "I was not aware that Poland has already decided to sign ACTA."

Nor were the NGO representatives in the room. After the shock wore off, they expressed outrage.

The Ministry of Economy official was surprised at the uproar he caused. He hadn't attended a Dialogue Group meeting before, and he had no clue that ACTA was such a hot-button item. Ostrowski even felt a little sorry for the official, who was a lower-level staff member not accustomed to dealing with such a hostile crowd.

The Ministry of Economy official tried to put a kibosh on the NGOs' dissent by informing them that it was too late to change the Prime Minister's decision to sign ACTA. ACTA was a done deal.

That angered the NGO reps even more. They told the government officials they would demand a public debate about ACTA, including in Parliament.

Trying to intervene, Ostrowski said that he planned on bringing the matter up with his boss, Minister of Administration and Digitization Michał Boni. Ostrowski vowed to do everything in his might to postpone the vote on ACTA.

The fight was on.

The meeting ended abruptly.

As he left the conference room, Deputy Minister Ostrowski understood how poorly the meeting went. It was a disaster. He immediately met with Minister Boni to discuss the lowlights of the meeting. Boni realized they had a major problem and said he would speak to Prime Minister Tusk to delay the signing of ACTA until the government had time to consider the concerns of the NGOs and the public.

That afternoon, Ostrowski tweeted the news of Boni's intended efforts to speak to the Prime Minister.[12] Boni would submit an official request, by letter, to the Prime Minister the next day to delay Poland's signing of ACTA.

Meanwhile, the NGO representatives fanned out from the meeting and started sounding the alarm about ACTA through all available means. A firestorm was brewing.

Outside the Prime Minister's Office, Piotr Waglowski, a prominent lawyer and leading Internet theorist in Poland, caught the attention of a news crew. Waglowski, who went by the name VaGla, was something akin to the Larry Lessig of Poland. VaGla was a founding member of the Information Society Poland and a leading lawyer who wrote influential articles about the Internet and intellectual property. In 2005, Poland awarded him a Cross of Merit for his contribution to the country's information infrastructure. VaGla told the reporter that Prime Minister Tusk was signing ACTA next week without any public consultations. VaGla also recounted the meeting, blow-by-blow, on his popular blog.[13]

Michał Woźniak, the President of Poland's Free and Open Source Software Foundation, did the same on his blog that day after leaving the ACTA meeting.[14] A self-described "human rights in digital era hacktivist," who went by the nickname "Rysiek," Woźniak sported long hair and a beard that made him look every bit the part of a free spirit. He could easily fit in on the streets of Berkeley. Woźniak explained how the EU Parliament was where the public should concentrate its efforts because the EU Parliament still needed to approve ACTA, even if Poland signed the agreement.

Katarzyna Szymielewicz, a lawyer and co-founder of Panoptikon, an NGO devoted to privacy and electronic surveillance issues, also reported the ACTA meeting on Panoptikon's website that day. Katarzyna's post was ominously titled: "Does Poland Threaten to Censor the Internet in the Name of Copyright Protection?"[15] She began her post by mentioning the Wikipedia blackout, SOPA, and "laws that could limit freedom of expression on the Internet with ISPs acting as 'private police' who shall prosecute copyright infringement." ACTA was just as bad, in her view.

By the next day, ACTA had become a major news story in Poland, following on the heels of the SOPA protests. ACTA made the front page of *Gazeta Wyborcza*, the leading newspaper in Poland.[16]

The NGOs' extensive blog coverage of the government's decision to sign ACTA drew incredible traffic through the week and weekend. Woźniak's blog crashed and went down for a week after a link on Slashdot to his blog post drove too much traffic to his site. Panoptikon's post on ACTA also crashed its server, requiring the NGO to create a mirror site to handle all the traffic, nearly 200,000 unique visitors a day, a record for the site.

At that moment, Katarzyna realized things were different. Maybe for the first time during her work for Panoptikon, many people and the mainstream media were actually interested in what the NGOs were reporting. Copyright, of all things, was a hot topic in Poland. Katarzyna sensed something big was about to happen.

*   *   *

By pure coincidence of events, the ACTA story got even bigger that day, thanks to the efforts of the U.S. government to shut down Megaupload, one of the most popular sites on the Internet, which at one point was the 13th most-trafficked site in the world. Megaupload was a service that allowed people to store files in a virtual "locker" and then create a link to share the file with others. The service was free, but in order to avoid wait periods to download the materials, Megaupload offered its users a premium account for $14. On the surface, there was nothing shady or illegal about the type of service Megaupload offered. Other sites like Dropbox offered a similar type of service, all on the up and up, giving users the ability to store content in the so-called cloud.

But, in an indictment disclosed in the United States on January 19, 2012, U.S. law enforcement charged that Megaupload was facilitating massive criminal copyright infringement of over $500 million in value, by basically being a Napster for movies and TV shows. The FBI and Department of Justice worked with New Zealand law enforcement to have Megaupload's founder, Kim Dotcom (aka Kim Schmitz), and six other executives arrested in New Zealand on January 20, 2012 for racketeering, money laundering, and criminal copyright infringement.

Pursuant to the PRO-IP Act, U.S. law enforcement seized the domain name Megaupload.com and shut down the site that day in what was aptly called Operation Takedown. In place of Megaupload, the U.S. government inserted its ominous "seizure" page—the same one that had triggered the idea for Fight for the Future's American Censorship Day—giving public notice of the shutdown of Megaupload. Given the time difference, news of Dotcom's arrest and Megaupload's shutdown were reported in both Europe and the United States on January 19, 2012, the day after the Wikipedia blackout. Of course, people who used Megaupload would find out about the shutdown immediately, in whatever time zone they lived.

The charges against Kim Dotcom and Megaupload would have to be proven in court, of course. But the extravagant lifestyle of Dotcom raised at least eyebrows, if not suspicion. At 6 feet 7 inches tall and over 300 pounds, Kim Dotcom, a 37-year-old German living in New Zealand, was a larger-than-life figure who enjoyed living life to the fullest. He leased the most expensive property in all of New Zealand, a 25,000 square foot mansion valued at $24 million that rented for over $24,000 a month.[17] He had three beds—including an official "work bed"—that were hand-crafted from Sweden, each costing $103,000 to make.[18] The New Zealand property included swimming pools, tennis courts, horse stables, and even realistic sculptures of giraffes and a rhinoceros. He also owned 15 Mercedes Benz cars, plus a $443,000 Rolls Royce Phantom Coupe with the license plate "God." Talk about vanity.

Dotcom maintained his innocence, however. Megaupload said its business was legitimate because it complied with the notice-and-takedown requirement of the U.S. DMCA safe harbor by removing unauthorized material upon receiving a notice from copyright holders. Before the arrest, Megaupload's business had the support of several famous U.S. celebrities, including Kanye West, will.i.am, P. Diddy, Chris Brown, Jamie Foxx, and even Kim Kardashian, all of whom recorded the catchy "Megaupload Song" video on YouTube.[19] Megaupload's CEO was hip hop producer Kaseem "Swizz Beatz" Dean, who was married to pop star Alicia Keyes—Dean was not arrested in the government's raid.

Whatever one's view of Dotcom, the New Zealand government's display of force in the copyright raid on January 20, 2012 seemed ill-conceived. Later that year, law enforcement would suffer several embarrassing setbacks. In June, a New Zealand court would rule that the warrants to seize Dotcom's property were too broad and therefore invalid, making the search and seizure illegal.[20] Then in September of that year, New Zealand Prime Minister John Key would personally apologize to Dotcom after an internal investigation revealed that law enforcement had used illegal electronic surveillance—or illegal spying—on Dotcom before the raid.[21] Despite these setbacks, the U.S. government still sought Dotcom's extradition to the United States, which a court in New Zealand was to decide in 2013. Meanwhile, Dotcom would later sue the New Zealand government for NZ$6 million for its illegal spying.

Even in January 2012, before any of these legal setbacks, the case against Megaupload didn't appear to be well-planned. The Department of Justice (DOJ) maintained that the timing of the shutdown of Megaupload and arrest of Dotcom on January 20, 2012 had nothing to do with the debate over SOPA, which had reached an inflection point in the January 18th Wikipedia blackout.[22] But that may have been part of the problem: DOJ appeared to be blind to the way in which the timing of its shutdown of Megaupload could affect, if not jeopardize, the U.S. government's efforts to get countries to sign ACTA. Indeed, January 20, 2012 in New Zealand—or January 19 in Europe—was probably the worst day imaginable.

In Poland, people learned about Dotcom's arrest and the shutdown of Megaupload just a day after the Wikipedia blackout had raised concerns about Internet policing under SOPA. That same day, they also learned that the Polish government would sign ACTA. Just when many people were nervous about—even fearful of—what the United States might do to the Internet under SOPA, U.S. law enforcement, in its crusade against piracy, shut down one of the most popular sites in the world.

First, SOPA and the Wikipedia blackout, then Megaupload's shutdown, and now Poland's plan to sign ACTA, all in the span of 48 hours. It was all too much: a perfect storm on the Internet.

The shutdown of Megaupload had the unintended consequence of stoking some Polish people's concerns about greater government policing of the Internet. For a country not too far removed from a totalitarian Communist regime, the thought of government-imposed policing of the Internet was downright frightening. As Woźniak from the Free and Open Source Software Foundation explained: "Poles still do remember vividly the communism years, police state, and censorship. And vehemently oppose any attempts of bringing them back in any form."[23]

People's interest in ACTA within Poland soon reached a fever pitch. As Mieszko Domagała, a high school student in Krakow who later participated in the street protests against ACTA, recounted, "The great popularity of Wikipedia and Megaupload drew the attention of many people who had never heard of ACTA."

Kuba Danecki, a Jagiellonian University student in Poland, added, "The Wikipedia blackout was a big thing. People really noticed something was going on. But the closing of Megaupload may have made people think even more. It was really awful timing for the ACTA supporters, especially after the blackout. It showed the single image of the Internet as a desert, where you can't find anything."

*   *   *

As news of the Prime Minister's decision to sign ACTA broke in Poland, Barbara Rogowska found the perfect topic for her next YouTube video. Rogowska was a comedy actress and theatre dresser, who had finally discovered her fifteen minutes of fame in her mid-fifties—on YouTube of all places.

Under her stage name Barbara Kwarc, Rogowska had become a huge YouTube celebrity in Poland, making videos of herself commenting on all sorts of issues ranging from culture to politics. With white hair, thin penciled-in eyebrows, prominent nose, and salty tongue, Kwarc was a cross between Phyllis Diller and Lisa Lampanelli. Kwarc's irreverent, sometimes vulgar humor was the reason for her incredible popularity. In three and a half years, Kwarc's YouTube videos amassed nearly 70 million views—double the size of the country's population. Like Justin Bieber, she commanded attention on YouTube, at least in Poland.

On Saturday, January 21, 2012, Kwarc, dressed in a military uniform and wearing dark aviator sunglasses, summoned her best General Wojciech Jaruzelski impersonation on YouTube.

Jaruzelski was the last Communist Prime Minister of Poland, who, on December 13, 1981, took to state TV and announced martial law in Poland. Wearing his decorated military uniform and staring from behind his thick plastic-framed glasses, Jaruzelski spoke slowly and calmly from a prepared speech to explain the reason for martial law.

"Citizens of the Polish People's Republic. I address you today as a soldier and as the head of the government of Poland," Jaruzelski began, looking straight into the camera, having memorized the opening line.[24] He spoke from a desk with a prepared text of the speech in front of him, and a prominent Polish flag in the background.

"Our country stands at the edge of an abyss. The achievements of many generations, the Polish house raised from the ashes, are collapsing. . . . The nation has reached the limits of mental endurance. Many people have been seized by despair. A national catastrophe is no longer days but only hours away. . . .

"It is today, precisely, that this must be announced, when we know the date of imminent, mass political demonstrations, some of them in the centre of Warsaw, to be organized in connection with the anniversary of the December events. . . .

"I hereby announce that today a Military Council of National Salvation has been constituted. In conformity with the provisions of the Constitution, the National Council will introduce at midnight tonight martial law throughout the country. . . . This is the ultimate step to start leading the country out of the crisis, to save the State from disintegration. . . . Before the entire Polish nation and the whole world I wish to repeat the immortal words: Poland has not yet perished, so long as we still live!"

Jaruzelski's infamous speech lasted only eight and a half minutes. But martial law in Poland lasted a year and a half, imposing military control over most facets of life including education, work, and the media. The period was a low point in Poland's history that left the country in economic shambles. The Solidarity resistance led by Lech Wałęsa, a charismatic trade union organizer who would later become Poland's first president, would take nearly a decade more to prevail in the quest for democracy in Poland.

In a YouTube video titled "Mr. Prime Minister, We are taking over control!," Kwarc flipped Jaruzelski's historic martial law speech on its head, invoking not repression, but Internet freedom.[25]

"Citizens and Internet users of Poland. I appeal to you today as the Queen of the Internet and a citizen of Poland," Kwarc said sternly, looking straight into the camera while wearing dark sunglasses as music appropriate for a military march played in the background. If she was reading from a monitor, you couldn't tell. Her delivery was flawless—even better than Jaruzelski's.

"The Internet faces a great danger. Achievements earned by generations of people, built on the heritage of Spectrum, Amiga,

Commodore, and Atari computers are being destroyed. . . . Our nation has reached its limits of mental strength. Many people suffer from sorrow and despair. In this moment, not days but hours separate us from global catastrophe. We need to announce it, especially today when we know a date for imminent mass demonstrations."

Kwarc's mention of impending demonstrations alluded to the street protests people were already planning in various cities of Poland through Facebook event pages. Her video itself helped to spur people to action.

"Citizens of Poland, I declare that today the Military Council of Internet Salvation constituted itself for the sake of us all. I, Barbara Kwarc, according to the Constitution of Poland, declare that today at midnight a martial law will come into force on the area of the whole Internet. I demand that this speech appear on all Internet websites and that all of you share it with your friends and family. Citizens of Poland, facing the whole world I would like to repeat these immortal words: Freedom for the Internet!"

The speech was incredible in its own right. But the spoof of General Jaruzelski added to its wide appeal. Instead of a bare desk, Kwarc sat behind a flag and a desk adorned with roses, a stuffed toy pig, giant plastic lips, and a smiling floppy dog sitting on top of a "Do Not Disturb" sign. The scene was outrageous.

Kwarc's video went viral, eventually getting over a million views.

And some of her viewers took her speech quite literally. Over the weekend, a group identifying itself as the Polish Underground hacked into Prime Minister Tusk's website and overtook it with a blacked-out page that included Kwarc's YouTube video declaring martial law for Internet freedom. Under a banner "Stop ACTA," the Polish Underground claimed responsibility and boasted about being bolder than the more well-known group Anonymous. The Polish Underground posted a message on the Prime Minister's site: "HACKED! STOP ACTA! Prime Minister Donald Tusk is a bad person! . . . You won't be censoring the Internet for us. You won't take away human rights!"[26]

The Polish Underground was trying to upstage Anonymous by

taking even more aggressive actions than Anonymous did. On January 22, 2012, Anonymous had announced on Twitter: "The Polish revolution is now beginning."[27] Anonymous engaged in denial-of-service attacks on several Polish government websites including the Chancellery of the Prime Minister and the Ministry of Culture. Anonymous threatened in a tweet: "We have dox files and leaked documentations on many Poland officials, if ACTA is passed, we will release these documents."[28]

A few days later, however, Anonymous called a ceasefire at the request or plea of Polish NGOs. Dealing with Anonymous, though, was no simple task. As the slogan went, Anonymous can be anyone. And they are legion. The group consisted of unnamed hacker-activists, or hacktivists, who used the Internet—such as through denial-of-service attacks and other online techniques—to protest entities, actions, or forces they disagreed with. Anonymous targeted a number of attacks against the websites of the U.S. government and the entertainment industry for their crusade against piracy, including during the SOPA debate and shutdown of Megaupload. Anonymous had plenty other targets of their protests, including the Church of Scientology, Sarah Palin, pedophiles, and the Westboro Baptist Church after it planned, in poor taste, to picket the funerals of the victims in the mass shooting at Sandy Hook School in Newtown, Connecticut. Anything that rubbed Anonymous the wrong way could be the target of its attack through the Internet. Beware.

Though its members were unknown, Anonymous was best known to the public by the symbol it adopted in its messages on Twitter and YouTube: the Guy Fawkes mask. Fawkes was a historical figure who was a part of the failed attempt to restore a Catholic monarch to the Crown by blowing up the House of Lords and assassinating King James in the Gunpowder Plot of 1605. Though Fawkes suffered an ignominious fate, jumping to his death before he could be hanged after he was tried as a traitor, he became somewhat of a legendary figure in Britain, which commemorates the foiling of the Gunpowder Plot each November 5th on what has come to be known as Guy Fawkes Day. The day is celebrated with bonfires and the burning of an effigy of someone disliked.

But most people today recognize the Guy Fawkes mask as the one worn by the character V in the 2005 movie *V for Vendetta*, based on a comic book's futuristic retelling—and revision—of the Guy Fawkes tale. Only this time, V is a hero who wears a Guy Fawkes mask as he fights for freedom against the totalitarian and oppressive regime of the British government. Ironically, Time Warner owns the copyright to the *V for Vendetta* mask and sells thousands of the masks each year, no doubt spurred by Anonymous's adoption of the mask as a symbol for its group. Neither Time Warner nor Anonymous seemed to mind.

In the murky world of Anonymous, it wasn't easy to know who Anonymous members were. Marcin "Sirmacik" Karpezo, a free culture activist and a member of Poland's Free and Open Source Software Foundation, along with a grad student named Tehora who specialized in econometrics and computer science, reached out to a foreign contact with connections to the Anonymous group. Through Internet Relay Chat, Sirmacik and Tehora spent over an hour trying to explain why they felt Anonymous's disruption of government websites was counterproductive to the NGOs' efforts. The attacks were only making the Prime Minister more determined to proceed forward with ACTA. As Tusk defiantly vowed in a press conference on January 24, 2012, the Polish government would not give in to "blackmail."[29]

Sirmacik and Tehora eventually convinced the foreign Anonymous contact to call for a cease fire. The Anonymous contact wrote a cease-fire statement in English with help and suggestions from Sirmacik and Tehora, who then translated it into Polish. The whole process took about an hour. On the same day of Prime Minister Tusk's remarks, the Anonymous contact posted both versions of the statement asking all Anonymous hacktivists in Poland to cease their cyber attacks on Polish government and EU websites.[30]

The notice worked. Within a few days, all attacks on the Polish government websites stopped.

But the Anonymous contact made it clear to Sirmacik: the NGOs had a few days to stop ACTA. If they failed, the Anonymous attacks would be back—and the cyber attacks against ACTA would be much bigger than before.

*   *   *

The NGOs had their work cut out for them. The weekend of January 21, 2012, they held emergency meetings to plan their response to the Polish government's decision to sign ACTA. On Sunday, Jarosław Lipszyc convened a meeting of the NGOs in Warsaw at his office at the Modern Poland Foundation, a nonprofit that digitized Polish public domain works for people and schools to share on the Internet, similar to the mission of Project Gutenberg.

Jarosław had quit his job of ten years as a journalist to work for Internet nonprofits and social causes. Writing about the world was not as exciting as changing the world, he believed. So, in 2006, he assumed the leadership of the Modern Poland Foundation. He also helped to start the Coalition for Open Education, which aimed to promote the development of open access materials for schools in Poland. Given his commitment to open access on the Internet, Jarosław had serious reservations about ACTA.

VaGla, Katarzyna, and Woźniak, the three activists from the January 19th ACTA meeting who were crucial in spreading the word about the government's decision through their blogs, also attended the meeting, as did other Internet activists and NGO representatives.

In some respects, the meeting resembled the Mozilla brown bag that organized American Censorship Day to protest SOPA in the United States back in November 2011. Like the Mozilla brown bag, the first thing the NGO group did was to agree to create a "Stop ACTA" email list to organize their efforts.

Next, the group discussed how to oppose ACTA. The group decided to write a letter to the government stating their objections to ACTA, both its content and the process in which it was negotiated. The letter was sent the next day.[31]

Jarosław then told the group that on his Facebook wall, some of his Facebook friends had already posted event pages to protest ACTA on the streets of Warsaw on Tuesday, January 24, 2012.

Others did the same in cities across Poland, but for January 25. The decision to protest was spontaneous and decentralized, conducted simply by people posting and sharing a Facebook event page.

Different from the SOPA protests in the United States, the Polish opposition focused on organizing live protests in the streets. Although Internet blackouts of Polish websites were also part of the protests, the real action occurred on the streets—in the cold and snow. Poland had a long history of mass demonstrations dating back to the 1980s with the Solidarity movement against the Communist government. Even with the change to a democratic government in 1990, street protests remained an integral part of Polish culture. If people had a common gripe, they protested on the streets. In droves. Now, with Facebook, organizing a protest was easy—and effective.

Wiktor Świątkowski, a law student and part-time worker for a web design company in Poland, had set up a Facebook fan page titled *Nie dla ACTA*, meaning "No to ACTA," back on June 17, 2010. Świątkowski, who went by the name "Wiktor Roktiw" (a combination of the palindrome of his first name), was interested in the free culture movement from his studies in law school. So he decided to track the debate over ACTA on a Facebook fan page, even though he was no fan of ACTA. Wiktor borrowed the catchy slogan "No to ACTA" popularized by the French Internet advocacy group La Quadrature du Net and other Internet nonprofits opposing ACTA. Then, on the pivotal day of January 19, 2012, after reading VaGla's blog post describing how the Polish government would sign ACTA, Wiktor decided to create a new Facebook event page devoted to ACTA. There was no official event, but Wiktor meant the page as a call to action for people to get involved in the debate and form their own view on ACTA. A million invitations were sent to people to join the event page, with eventually over 479,000 people signing up.

The next day, two other Poles, Andrzej Tucholski and Arkadiusz Lech, created a similar page titled *Nie dla ACTA w Polsce* ("No to ACTA in Poland") that eventually had nearly 200,000 "likes."[32] Tucholski, a student at the University of Warsaw, explained to the

Polish media why they got involved: "As we wrote in the information on the Facebook fan page, 'We do not like vague laws.' The fan page was created primarily to inform people about the ambiguities and our doubts about the ACTA agreement."[33]

Another Facebook page made a direct connection to the SOPA debate by titling the page: *Nie dla ACTA SOPA PIPA – Krakow*, meaning "No to ACTA, SOPA, PIPA – Krakow."[34]

Other people on Facebook soon created event pages to hold protests against ACTA across Poland. Bartłomiej Świstak Piotrowski, a 27-year-old who provided social network consulting for businesses, organized the Krakow protest event page on Facebook.[35] His Facebook event page was set for January 25 and eventually had over 85,000 invites to people, with over 28,000 people saying they would attend. Numerous other Facebook pages set up protests for other cities in Poland.

At the Sunday meeting at Modern Poland Foundation's office, the representatives of the various NGOs decided to join the Warsaw protest announced on Facebook instead of holding a separate event. Some of the NGO reps didn't think that their role included organizing protests, so they decided that their responsibility should be to provide legal analysis of ACTA to the media and public. Other reps decided to contact the organizers of the Facebook event and try to help out with the planned protest in Warsaw, including securing the necessary city permit to hold a public demonstration.

A key decision the protest organizers made was to keep the protests free of logos or banners from political parties—a practice that would be replicated in other cities and countries. The protest message might be undermined if it were co-opted by one of Poland's political parties, liberal or conservative. People were fighting for Internet freedom, not a political party.

* * *

Warsaw was the site of the first ACTA protest. Many people in Poland felt it was fitting for Warsaw, the capital of Poland, to lead the way, to fire the first shot at ACTA. On Tuesday,

January 24, 2012, over a thousand people convened in front of the local EU Parliament office on a cold, wintry day.

Jarosław feared that the protest might be a flop. But when he arrived, he was surprised—and ecstatic—by the turnout, not only the large number but also the composition. Students. Scores of students, both college and high school students. It was a sight to behold.

The students had grown up with the Internet and spent much of their time using the Internet for their daily activities and access to culture, perhaps even more so than older adults. Although Poland was considered a developed country, it was one of the poorest in that category. At the time, Poland had a high unemployment rate of 12.5%. Despite the difficult economic conditions, nearly 64% of Polish households had Internet access in 2010, while college students had access through their universities. Most students and young adults in Poland didn't have luxuries, but they did have the Internet.

As Mieszko Domagała, a high school student at ZSE (School of Energy), who helped to round up people for the January 25, 2012 protest in Krakow, explained, "I spend a lot of time on the Internet. I use the Internet almost always. At school, at work, at home, by PC or smartphone." Domagała joined the protest organization because he wanted to protect the Internet, which provided people with access to culture and learning.

People viewed ACTA's potential to impose greater policing of the Internet as a threat to their daily existence. The fear of ACTA among Internet users was captured best by a cute cartoon posted on one of the "Stop ACTA" Polish event pages on Facebook. The cartoon had a drawing of a poor animal standing in the rain, with ears drooping and the caption: "Dear ACTA, I have no boyfriend nor girlfriend. The Internet is all I have. Please don't take it away from me."

"No to ACTA! No to ACTA! No to ACTA!" people chanted in unison on the streets of Warsaw.

The atmosphere at the protest was boisterous, but orderly. Some people wore Anonymous masks, while others taped their mouths with the word "ACTA" written on the tape as a form of self-censorship.

Spontaneously, the crowd started jumping in place, borrowing a popular cheer from soccer games.

Kto nie skacze, ten za ACTA! Kto nie skacze, ten za ACTA!

Who does not jump supports ACTA! Who does not jump supports ACTA!

Of course, no one there supported ACTA, so everybody jumped, and jumped, and jumped. The jumping was infectious and spread across the crowd like a wave. Some people captured on video the frenetic scene of hundreds of people jumping up and down, and posted it on YouTube. Someone even brought a laptop to play Barbara Kwarc's "Internet freedom" video.[36] It was a raucous scene. The crowd was so energized.

The jumping was also a good way for people to generate some body heat on that freezing cold January evening. Ultimately, the protest lasted a little over an hour. It was a huge success, serving as the opening salvo against ACTA.

The next day, a wave of protests swept through Poland in cities and towns, big and small. They followed the same script as the Warsaw protest, starting with their organization on Facebook and including some of the same chants—and jumping.

The largest and most dramatic protest occurred in Krakow, where over 15,000 people filled the streets of the main square. Krakow was a university city, home to ten colleges and universities, with a student population of over 170,000, or roughly 20% of the total population. The protest started at six o'clock in the evening and lasted ninety minutes. Temperatures were frigid, dropping to -5 degrees Celsius (23 degrees Fahrenheit). But people still came, eager to protest.

As in Warsaw, students in Krakow turned out in large numbers, as did many other people from the city. Jacek Smoter, a student and a photojournalist for a local website "Love Krakow," was impressed by the massive turnout of people from diverse backgrounds. As he was snapping photos of the mammoth crowd, he passed an older gentleman, probably in his 60s, who remarked: "Take as many photos as possible because you won't see that many people in one place again in your life."

Smoter was moved by the old man's words. The gentleman had witnessed the Solidarity protests in the 1980s, so his comment about the protest carried credibility. Smoter did his best to capture the historic night in his photos, which conveyed the beauty of the throng of protesters overflowing on the streets of Krakow. Illuminated in the background were the Town Hall Tower and the majestic Renaissance Sukiennice, a majestic structure built in the 13th century as a marketplace.[37] With such architectural beauty providing the stage, the protests in Krakow were breathtaking.

And awe-inspiring. Thousands of people filling the streets jumped up and down in unison, as someone with a megaphone led them in the soccer chant of "Who does not jump supports ACTA." The scene from Krakow may have been the most impressive of all the protests against ACTA throughout Europe.

Kuba Danecki, a college student who helped organize the protest, was astonished by the large turnout in Krakow. Serving as security at the protest to keep it orderly, he couldn't believe how long the line of protesters stretched on the streets of the Main Square. The line snaked back for nearly a mile. The protesters marched all the way to the office of Jerzy Miller, the representative of the national government in Krakow. The protesters intended to deliver a petition against ACTA, which they planned on posting to the office door *à la* Martin Luther. But some late worker in Miller's office spared the protesters the dramatic delivery and received the petition by hand.

The crowd was so large that it was hard for the throng of people to navigate the narrow Florianska Gate, built in medieval times as the entrance to the Old Town. The gate could fit only a few people at a time, so it created a human traffic jam near the end of the march.

It was still too early to tell the fallout from the fast-moving events. In just three days of protests, over fifty cities in Poland demonstrated against ACTA.

Afterwards, Deputy Minister Ostrowski reflected on the historic protests, "January 25 was the day I realized the power of the Internet."

Along with others in the Polish government, Ostrowski had been monitoring the protests. Although he didn't participate in the protests, others in the government associated the protests with Ostrowski and thought he was a troublemaker of sorts, a "Minister ACTA." Ostrowski didn't mind the derision from his colleagues because the protests against ACTA were far more important than what others thought about him.

"We saw, for the first time, maps with red all over the country," Ostrowski explained. The red stood for all the protest sites. Unlike past protests in Poland, where only one city or a few cities might participate, the ACTA protests spanned the country in large cities and small towns. The entire country of Poland had turned red, against ACTA.

In January 2012, people had no way of knowing how severely the protests in Poland damaged ACTA's chances of ratification in the EU. Only time would later show just how devastating the Polish protests were. Like a virus, they would spread rapidly across Europe and debilitate ACTA.

Chapter 6

Hello, Democracy

On January 26, 2012, the EU's signing of ACTA took place as planned in Tokyo. The EU Commission (the EU's executive body) signed, as did most countries of the EU. Jadwiga Rodowicz-Czechowska, the former actress who was the Polish ambassador to Japan, did the honor for Poland. Only Germany, Cyprus, Estonia, the Netherlands, and Slovakia didn't sign the agreement. Germany's omission was significant, given its importance as an economic power in the EU. The Japanese foreign affairs ministry tried to downplay the omission, maintaining that Germany and the four other EU countries were expected to sign ACTA upon "the completion of respective domestic procedures."[1]

That never came to fruition. ACTA would soon be derailed by mass demonstrations in every country of the EU.

In Poland, the climate was volatile as more street protests were planned. Someone wrote a call to action on the "No to ACTA" Facebook event page: "Dear compatriots! Internet Queen Barbara Kwarc announced a few days ago the state of war. Join in her words, because tonight ACTA was signed."[2]

In Poland's Parliament, over 30 members from the leftist Palikot party wore paper Anonymous masks as a display of opposition to ACTA. However, many of the Polish Internet NGOs and ACTA street protesters viewed the Palikot "Anonymous" masks as a publicity stunt by politicians.

A day later, on January 27, 2012, Kader Arif, a French minister to the EU Parliament, abruptly resigned as the European Parliament's rapporteur for ACTA. Arif's responsibility was to serve as the liaison for the EU Parliament in the ACTA negotiations, but he had finally had enough.

"I will not participate in this charade," Arif declared in a statement on his website. "I want to denounce as the greatest of all the process that led to the signing of this agreement: no association of civil society, lack of transparency from the beginning of negotiations, successive postponements of the signing of the text without any explanation being given, setting aside the claims of the European Parliament expressed in several resolutions of our Assembly."[3]

ACTA was quickly becoming unhinged. The popular uprising against ACTA in Poland soon started a chain reaction, first in Poland and then in other parts of Europe.

On February 3, 2012, in a dramatic turnabout, Prime Minister Donald Tusk announced that Poland was suspending its ratification of ACTA until at least the end of 2012.[4] Tusk even conceded that the consultations with the public on ACTA had not been sufficient, and it was possible that Poland would reject ACTA. Tusk didn't become the longest-serving Prime Minister of Poland without being politically astute. The people had spoken against ACTA on the streets in cities throughout Poland. It would be political suicide for him to ignore their complaints.

In a remarkably candid press conference, Tusk even admitted being too old in his view about the Internet. "I must admit that the discussion on copyright, property rights, rights of the users, and the right to access, particularly to cultural and public information, all requires discussion on an incomparably higher level than before. Maybe because of when I was born, I approached this issue from a very twentieth-century point of view. But the next level means meeting the demands of the twenty-first century. We need to catch up."

Tusk proposed a public meeting on ACTA, as well as a reexamination of Poland's copyright law to make it more flexible for the Internet age. Like some of the SOPA sponsors did during the January 18th Wikipedia blackout, Tusk made a complete about-face.

Tusk's switch from supporting to opposing ACTA seemed like a religious conversion. On February 6, 2012, Tusk held a public consultation about ACTA that lasted seven hours straight—miraculously without any lunch or bathroom breaks.[5]

Among the government officials in attendance were Ostrowski and Boni from the Ministry of Digitization, Minister of Culture Zdrojewski, and Deputy Minister of Culture Piotr Żuchowski. Three hundred fifty people from NGOs and various stakeholder groups were invited to attend in person, and the public was invited to participate over Internet Relay Chat. Tusk and the other government officials openly fielded questions about ACTA from the audience and over the Internet. The meeting was broadcast in real time on the Internet, Polish radio, and TV, and was later posted in a video on YouTube.[6]

The marathon session was a victory for the Internet NGOs and, indeed, Poland's democracy—a watershed moment. The questions and answers were frank and completely unfiltered. The public consultation helped to spark the formation of the Congress of the Freedom on the Internet in Poland, a group consisting of several ad hoc task forces with members from government and the private sector. The task forces would prepare reports on a number of key issues relating to the Internet, including copyright reform.

A couple weeks later, Tusk went one step further by writing a letter asking his fellow European People's Party (EPP) leaders, including German Chancellor Angela Merkel and the heads of state of other EU countries, to reject ACTA.[7]

Like a confession, Tusk described his letter in a press conference that day: "I was wrong. . . . It would be a sin to maintain a mistaken belief."

The mea culpa sounded sincere, a rarity for politicians.

"The ACTA agreement does not correspond to the reality of the 21st century. The battle for the right to property should also respect the right to freedom."

Poland's suspension of its ratification of ACTA had a domino effect in other countries. Within less than a week, Germany, Bulgaria, the Czech Republic, Latvia, and Slovakia all announced they were suspending the signing or ratification of ACTA in their respective countries. A week later, the EU Commission, which had negotiated ACTA on behalf of the EU, referred the matter to the Court of Justice of the European Union to determine if ACTA violated fundamental rights protected by EU law. The Commission's strategy may have been to buy time to delay the vote in the EU Parliament and let the protests die down, so ACTA could be passed at a more hospitable time. But if that was the strategy, it didn't work.

*   *   *

As the January street protests against ACTA in Poland erupted, Sebastian Radtke had mixed emotions in Germany. Radtke, an IT professional living in the small town of Kassel situated in the middle of Germany, had been helping to organize a mass protest against ACTA in Germany and other countries of Europe since January 14, 2012. He read news of the Polish protests on Google News and saw dramatic photos of the thousands of people who protested in the streets. He was inspired by the thousands of people in Poland who protested ACTA on the streets during the cold of January. But he was also embarrassed.

They're already protesting in Poland, Radtke thought to himself. *Faul.* We're *lazy* and do nothing.

We need to do something now, he resolved. Germany can't be left behind. We must join the fight.

Radtke was an accidental activist of sorts. With a background in graphic design and IT, Radtke hadn't been one to devote his time to political causes. His biggest passion at the time was video games. He was an avid gamer since the age of seven. Some 26 years later, his library of video games numbered over 700. The boxes and cases for the games lined the nearly six-foot high bookshelf in Radtke's flat. Along with many others in the gaming community, Radtke had eagerly awaited the release of *Battlefield 3* in the fall of 2011. The war game created by the U.S. company Electronic Arts had state-of-the-art graphics and animations of warfare. As EA pitched it, *Battlefield 3* enabled "unrivaled destruction."[8]

Battlefield 3 may have done even more, though. German gamers alleged that the "Origin," a third-party service for *Battlefield 3* that was necessary to play the game on PCs, operated as spyware tracking the users' computer activities and then sharing the information with third parties. *Gamestar* magazine published an article on October 25, 2011 with analysis by German lawyer Thomas Schwenke, who concluded that EA's end user license agreement (EULA), which authorized this kind of tracking, violated German privacy law.[9]

The story erupted when the popular German publication *Spiegel* ran a story online about the EA controversy a few days later. The story included Schwenke's analysis, as well as a similar conclusion drawn by Thomas Hoeren, a judge and professor of the Faculty of Law at the University of Münster.[10]

The EA spyware controversy sparked Radtke to action. He started following the controversy on his blog, which he converted from just a personal blog to a blog dedicated to the *Battlefield 3* controversy. By coincidence—or perhaps destiny—Radtke's personal blog was called "The Origin," a gamer nickname he had been using for nearly 15 years. So, if anyone was meant to cover the Origin controversy, it was Radtke.

Within 48 hours of covering the controversy, Radtke's blog, TheOrigin.de, went viral and had over 40,000 unique daily visitors during the height of the controversy. Before that, Radtke's blog had attracted only a handful of friends. Radtke had to upgrade his blog software in order to handle all the traffic.

Almost overnight, Radtke went from gaming hobbyist to political activist. He helped to organize a meeting in Cologne with high-level EA executives. The meeting didn't resolve all of the issues raised by the gaming community, but Radtke and the other representatives believed progress had been made in getting EA to understand their privacy concerns.

More important for the ACTA debate, the *Battlefield 3* controversy was transformative for Radtke and his new-found activism. Much in the way that the Grey Tuesday protest was formative to Fight for the Future's later efforts against SOPA, Radtke's experience in opposing EA's use of the Origin spyware was a critical learning experience that prepared him for the fight against ACTA. Through the EA *Battlefield 3* experience, Radtke developed skills at building an online campaign through his blog, which continued to draw at least 5,000 unique visitors each day. Almost by accident, he became a political activist on Internet issues in Germany.

And as fate would have it, Radtke's activism coincided with the SOPA debate in the United States. Sometimes, timing *is* everything. The confluence—or coincidence—of events could not have been more fortuitous for the opposition to ACTA. The SOPA protests proved to be like forest fires. Once they started, they quickly spread—even across the Atlantic.

Radtke reached out to Holmes Wilson from Fight for the Future to see how people in Germany could help to stop SOPA. Holmes was happy to offer his advice. When their discussion turned to ACTA, Holmes was stoked about the possibility that the SOPA protests might have a ripple effect on ACTA and get people in Europe to protest there.

It was like getting two for the price of one, Holmes mused.

Radtke started blogging about the SOPA debate on December 19, 2011 and then spread the word about the upcoming blackout to get German websites to join. In a post titled "ACTA and SOPA," he painted an ominous picture of what life would be like under the two controversial laws: "On every corner our rights are being eroded and cut, it is this vast web of laws for only one purpose: The control of the Internet, the last bastion of free speech and uncensored information."[11]

Radtke found hope in the White House's declaration against SOPA on January 14, 2012, and he anticipated the impending Internet blackout. "We will set an example and depending on how many sites are involved, this day could go down in history. The first day for over 20 years where the Internet stops," he wrote.

January 18, 2012 didn't go as far as shutting down the Internet, but the day was every bit as historic. Radtke blacked out his own site, while other sites like the German Wikipedia joined the many websites in the United States that were protesting SOPA.

During January 2012, Radtke also started to follow closely the debate over ACTA in Europe after reading an article on the Internet about the controversy. He had a chance meeting with Thumay Karbalai Assad, the chairman of the Pirate Party in Hessen, Germany, at a social gathering after the New Year. Radtke asked whether the Party was doing anything about ACTA.

"No, nothing," Karbalai Assad replied.

"We need to do something," Radtke suggested. "We should organize an opposition to ACTA."

"OK, why don't you take the lead?"

Radtke should have been careful what he wished for—he would become a "node" through which many of the protest organizers in numerous cities in Germany and other European Union countries would coordinate their efforts. Although each city had organizers on the ground, Radtke and a team of five other Germans provided logistical support and oversight to make sure each city had a blueprint for the protests. The group included Karbalai Assad and Thomas Gaul, the Vice Political Leader of the Pirate Party in Germany's Nordhessen region, who provided critical connections to other organizers across Europe.

The Pirate Party was a political movement started by the charismatic tech entrepreneur Rick Falkvinge in Sweden on January 1, 2006, the date when the party's website went live. In the digital age, a political party didn't exist until it was on the Internet. Falkvinge, who started his first company when he was sixteen, likened the Pirate Party's origin to founding a startup. He had registered the domain name "piratepartiet.se" only a few weeks before the site's launch because he saw an opportunity to start something special. "Changes to the available technology tend to drive political movements, rather than the other way around," Falkvinge explained. "You can see that in many cases throughout history." The Internet was simply the next frontier.

Sweden was also home to The Pirate Bay, a website for sharing movies, music, and other files through BitTorrent file-sharing software. The Pirate Bay was public enemy No. 1 to Hollywood, which filed a criminal complaint against the site for copyright infringement in 2004 that led to the police raid of The Pirate Bay's offices and eventual conviction and imprisonment of the founders of the site in Sweden. The Pirate Party wasn't affiliated with The Pirate Bay, but Falkvinge was appalled by the heavy-handed tactics used against the website.

Although the name of the Pirate Party smacked of lawlessness and illegality, it symbolized the group's effort to subvert the content industry's "war on piracy" into a referendum on reforming copyright law for the Internet age. As the UK Pirate Party explained on its website, "our name was gifted to us by the very organisations which we oppose."[12]

In a TEDx talk before a packed Sadler's Wells Theatre in London, Falkvinge explained the Party's mission: "Basically, we love the Net. We love copying and sharing. And we love civil liberties. For that, some people call us pirates. And, rather than being shamed by this, which I think was their intent, we decided to stand tall about it."[13]

Within a few short years, Pirate Parties sprouted in more than 60 countries, with the Pirate Parties International, an NGO, helping to coordinate their mission. By 2012, the Pirate Party was the fastest growing party in Europe: it had quickly gained two seats in the EU Parliament, 15 seats in the German Parliament, and more than 150 seats in local councils across Europe. In Sweden, the Party even commanded the largest number of voters under the age of 30. A revolution was afoot.

Although the Pirate Party had a comprehensive platform ranging from protecting the environment to promoting equality, its position on copyright was the one it was most famous for. The Party sought a copyright reform that would enable greater free access to culture: "[C]opying, providing access to, storing and using creative products for non-commercial purposes must not just be legalized, but actively promoted to improve the public availability of information, knowledge and culture because this is a prerequisite for the social, technological and economic development of our society."[14]

Even though Radtke's group had affiliations with the Pirate

Party, they felt it was important to participate in their personal capacities, similar to how the Polish protests were free of political parties. The ACTA protests weren't a Pirate Party production— instead, they were organized and carried out by people who cared about the Internet.

Radtke's group took on a sense of urgency right after the dramatic protests in Poland. Similar to Radtke's reaction, Karbalai Assad was spurred to action after watching YouTube videos of the Polish protests. Lying in bed, watching the videos on his smartphone on the last Sunday of January 2012, he was floored. He hadn't been closely following the ACTA debate. But he suddenly became interested then. How could Poland bring out so many protesters to the streets? And why wasn't the German media reporting more about ACTA?

We must act now, Karbalai Assad resolved, thinking about his 16-year-old daughter whose freedoms on the Internet he wanted to see protected.

ACTA was a Trojan horse, in his view. It didn't look so bad on the surface, but once it was accepted, it would open up the Internet to further restrictions sought by the content industry, which would come rushing in like the Greeks at the Battle of Troy. His fears found some support in the justifications some SOPA supporters had used when arguing in favor of domain name blocking based on the existence of comparable techniques used by other countries and the United States.

What angered Karbalai Assad the most was that ACTA was negotiated behind closed doors, without any opportunity for public debate. So people must take the debate to the streets.

He tweeted in German: "@Piratenpartei #Piraten Who would like to help me to organize national anti- #ACTA protests in Germany? /cc @theorigin79."[15] Three people replied back on Twitter, agreeing to be a part of a planning group in Germany that would help coordinate protests throughout the EU.

On the weekend of January 28, 2012, Radtke and Karbalai Assad convened the group to make the protests against ACTA a top priority. They decided the earliest date they could possibly hold a protest was February 11, a Saturday two weeks away. They wanted to protest as soon as possible to keep the media attention on ACTA following the Polish protests. But, realistically, they knew they needed time for planning and coordination among the various cities and countries of the EU.

After the first protests in Poland, their objective was clear: get thousands of people all around Europe to protest ACTA on the same day—and get the mainstream media to report it. The formula was simple. It was similar to the idea hatched by Fight for the Future to protest SOPA on American Censorship Day, which in turn provided the template for the January 18th Wikipedia blackout. But, unlike the SOPA protests, which occurred mainly online, the ACTA protests were all about hitting the pavement in massive numbers. Organizing a mass demonstration in one country was no small undertaking, but Poland had already pulled it off. Organizing protests in over 250 cities and 27 countries in 2 weeks, however, was a tall order. A Kilimanjaro.

But the Internet was a godsend to their cause. The group set up a wiki website at wiki.stoppacta-protest.info, which, along with Facebook event pages, would operate as the organizing tool for the protest organizers to plan and report their efforts from various countries. Kai Möller of the Pirate Party in Hessen, Germany set up the wiki and provided IT support. The wiki linked to a "Stop ACTA" website run by members of the Pirate Party who had been following the controversy for several years.[16] The organizers posted all the information for the protests on the "Stop ACTA" wikis, which centralized the protest details for all countries in one place. Access Now, an international human/digital rights organization founded after the Iranian protests during the Arab Spring in 2009, did the same on its website, listing all the Facebook event pages for the protests.

Pirate Party members provided outreach through their numerous contacts and channels via Twitter and email to find a volunteer from each country or region to serve as the point person for organizing the street protests there. Each protest organizer received a "Pirate pad," a Web-based app that allowed people to collaborate simultaneously in a document, similar to how Google Docs allowed Wikimedia staff to prepare for the January 18th blackout.

The protest organizers also set up Facebook event pages for the protests in their regions, in order to spread the word. If you wanted to reach young people in Europe, all you had to do was go on Facebook. That's where they hung out. As the Polish protests had already showed, the social network proved to be an indispensable way to publicize the protests and get bodies to the streets. The organizers also needed to make sure to secure the necessary permits in Germany and elsewhere to hold demonstrations on the streets.

Many of the organizers from the various cities reported daily to Radtke, who made sure everyone was on the same page and had the necessary support. The volume of communications was enormous. Radtke received over 8,000 emails and held 300 conferences online, with calls to the field organizers typically lasting several hours each night. In the final two weeks before the protest, Radtke worked round the clock, getting only a few hours' sleep when he could.

Only once did Radtke despair that the organization wouldn't make the February 11th protest date. The group needed to print up 10,000 flyers for the protests with translations into different languages, and then to ship them out to the organizers in the field. It was an enormous production requiring at least five business days. Radtke knew they would be cutting it close. Luckily, with financial support from the Pirate Party and private backers, the flyers were delivered in time.

Radtke's group was just a small part of the sprawling opposition to ACTA. There were many others involved in the fight throughout the EU. German nonprofit Digitale Gesellschaft, founded by Internet activist/blogger Markus Beckedahl, and many other volunteers were instrumental to the effort to stop ACTA. Beckedahl even blogged about how they built an anti-ACTA campaign, including the preparation of protest signs, flyers, stickers, and bags to hand out to protesters in various cities.[17] Other NGOs in Europe—including the Belgium-based European Digital Rights (EDRi) and Access Now, Open Rights Group in the UK, and Bits of Freedom in the Netherlands—also provided important contributions to the opposition to ACTA.

The vast number of people involved in stopping ACTA underscored a simple fact about the protests—ultimately, no one was in control. It was a free for all, with people contributing their own part to the cause.

But that's what made the opposition so effective, just as it was in the case of the SOPA protests. As La Quadrature du Net's co-founder Jérémie Zimmermann put it, "One of the keys to winning this victory was the multitude and the multiplicity of channels of action."

Meanwhile, at the end of January 2012, the EU Commission, the executive for the EU that signed ACTA, made a desperate effort to salvage the PR battle over ACTA following the Polish protests. The Commission published a list of "Ten Myths About ACTA," with counterpoints explaining why they were wrong.[18] By then, though, the PR battle for the EU Commission was just about lost.

When February 11, 2012 finally arrived, Radtke was tired and relieved. The organization for the protest was in place. Many people across Europe had worked tirelessly over the past two weeks to make the ACTA protest possible in 27 different countries. Radtke took pride in being a part of the grassroots movement. The only thing left to do now was to go to the protest—and see who else showed up.

When Radtke arrived at the protest site in his town's center, he couldn't believe his eyes. The place was packed. Never before had he seen the small town center teeming with people. Approximately 1,500 people showed up.

The crowd was so large it shut down traffic in the town center, although the organizers had secured the necessary permit from the local authorities to hold the protest there. Radtke brought his laptop and camera to the protest, and received updates from the other organizers who reported live protest numbers from their various locations. He entered the data into a spreadsheet, which he circulated to the press afterwards with the help of Kine Haasler, who was handling press relations.

When it was Radtke's turn to speak over the megaphone, he was energized and excited by the crowd, despite his lack of sleep over the past couple of weeks.

"In all of Germany, thousands of people are on the streets, and if you have a look to the left and right, you will see a lot of strangers. But nevertheless they are all here for one reason, there is one thing that connects us: We are standing here for our rights, our freedom and our democracy.… Representatives of the content industry and lobbyists developed ACTA behind closed doors. But how can such a system of rules dictate the fortunes of hundreds of thousands of people, if not even millions worldwide?"[19]

Just a few months ago, Radtke couldn't have imagined himself helping to lead a political movement. But after *Battlefield 3*, he knew his mission.

"The formulations in ACTA are vague and give a lot of room for speculations, but between the lines and in footnotes you can read: imposing Internet Service Provider responsibility, Internet censorship and self-censorship because people are afraid of things that could happen when ACTA takes place. Don't get us wrong— we are also for a fair payment of artists and creators, and we are against software piracy. But we don't support old ways of thinking that expired years ago and don't fit into the 21st century anymore and which don't fit into our information age."

The street protesters in Kassel cheered loudly with approval.

At that moment, Radtke was so proud of his small town of Kassel, he could barely contain his emotions. "We are standing here for our right of democracy, for freedom of expression and for a free Internet. Thank you, Kassel—you are marvelous!"

*   *   *

All around Europe, scenes similar to the one in Kassel were playing out on that historic day. The protests swept across Europe. Organizers prepared a Google map with pins on all the cities where protests were to be held with links to the Facebook events pages for the protests.[20] The map looked like a battlefield, with civilian troops mobilized all throughout Europe. Over 250 cities throughout Europe held protests against ACTA.

Germany had the greatest participation. Over 55 cities joined the protest. In the largest cities, people hit the streets in droves. Munich had an estimated 20,000 protesters; Berlin, 10,000; Hamburg, 8,000; and Stuttgart, 6,500. Karbalai Assad attended the protest in Frankfurt and was overjoyed by the huge crowd of 6,000 people who joined.

France also had a strong showing, with over 45 cities holding demonstrations against ACTA, including a thousand people in Paris. The work of French nonprofit La Quadrature du Net, which had been tracking and fighting against ACTA from the start, was crucial to the opposition. An important source of information and activism during the ACTA debate, the group created a "pi" phone on its website using voice over IP, so that visitors to the website could use the Internet and call the Members of the EU Parliament who were still possibly supporting ACTA. The phone system was similar to the successful feature Tumblr used on American Censorship Day.

In parts of Central and Eastern Europe, the numbers were just as impressive. The turnout in Romania was surprisingly robust, with 40 cities participating in the protest. Cluj-Napoca had over 2,000 protesters, which was even larger than the gathering in Bucharest, the capital and largest city of Romania. The great turnout was due to the large number of students in Cluj, which hosts Romania's largest university. CreativeMonkeyz, a popular comic animation site based out of Cluj, helped to spread the word about ACTA by posting a five-minute educational video about ACTA and its threat to the Internet.[21] The video was visually arresting in a way reminiscent of Fight for the Future's viral video against SOPA.

On the day of the protest, a few thousand people, many of them college students, marched on the streets of Cluj-Napoca in below-freezing temperatures. Many wore paper Anonymous masks they had purchased online. Others taped their mouths with "ACTA" printed on the tape. To keep warm, people jumped up and down, shouting the soccer chant in Romanian: "Whoever doesn't jump does not want change." The scene resembled the protests in Poland.

Other protesters chanted: "You shout ACTA, we shout ENOUGH! You signed ACTA, we will not forget it. ACTA, do not forget, we are your censor."

Two young Romanian protesters, one wearing an Anonymous mask, even held up a sign written in English with the words "ACTA, SOPA-PIPA" crossed out and a warning to Hollywood: "This revolution will NOT be televised." Another held up a sign stating: "Paws off the Internet."

Laura Muresan, a 24-year-old photojournalist who was getting a master's in media production, served as a citizen reporter for CNN at the Cluj-Napoca protest. Muresan captured the historic protest in her photographs and CNN iReport. She estimated that 90% of the protesters were young and were marching for "freedom on the Internet."[22]

The dramatic march proceeded from the Union Square at the centre of Cluj-Napoca towards the Prefecture Palace, a majestic castle-like building, then to the baroque-style City Hall, and finally back to the Square. The protest began in the daytime but ended after nightfall, lasting some three hours. It was remarkable.

Bulgaria also had a big turnout, with 16 cities participating in the protest. The capital, Sofia, had over 5,000 people demonstrate in an especially boisterous protest that proceeded from the National Palace of Culture all the way to Parliament. The march was captured in a popular YouTube video that drew tens of thousands of views.[23] At the head of the line, Bulgarian protesters carried a massive sign that read: "ACTA LA VISTA, BABY," a reference to Arnold Schwarzenegger's famous line from *Terminator 2*. In the minds of the protesters, ACTA was about to be terminated.

Maya Nikolova, one of the protesters in Sofia, told a news reporter what the fight was about: "I am here because I am against censorship on the Internet, against the attempts to limit the freedom of information and against corporate interests which trample human rights."[24]

Nikolova's remark pretty much summed up why so many

people were protesting ACTA throughout Europe that day.

There were a few disappointments, though. In the United Kingdom, only seven cities participated. In London, the United Kingdom's largest city, only a few hundred joined the protest in the city centre. Italy and Portugal also had only a few cities participate, with relatively small turnouts for the protests.

Even with sparse turnout in some cities, the protests were an overwhelming success. All told, the event organizers estimated that over 120,000 people marched on the streets against ACTA on that day.[25] What made the numbers even more remarkable were the cold temperatures—well below freezing in many places. All around Europe, people marched on the streets, many carrying signs stating "No to ACTA" and "Free Internet." Many people wore Anonymous masks or taped their mouths shut. Others came armed with cameras and cellphones, and posted photos and videos of the protests on Facebook and YouTube. The street protesters in Mainz, Germany even prepared a video of thanks to the protesters in Poland for leading the way against ACTA. The video itself received over a half million views on YouTube.[26]

Back in Kassel, Radtke went home ecstatic over the day's events. His body couldn't muster any energy to celebrate, though. As soon as he got home, he plopped down on his bed and fell asleep, feeling for the first time that ACTA would fail to pass in the EU Parliament. It was the first good sleep he had in two weeks. Sweet dreams.

February 11, 2012 was a historic display of civic activism in the 27 countries of the European Union. The protests achieved their objective. The major media outlets throughout Europe and abroad reported the controversy and popular opposition to ACTA. The scenes of thousands of people protesting ACTA in the streets in over 250 cities of Europe left an indelible impression in the popular debate: shock and awe—and jumping.

Although a vote on ACTA in the EU Parliament wouldn't take place until the summer, the February 11th protest had turned the tide of popular opinion against the trade agreement. As one person tweeted, "Seems like the people really don't like ACTA."[27]

For good measure, street protests were held again throughout Europe on February 25 and June 9, though with smaller turnouts. By then, ACTA was a dead act walking.

*   *   *

Leaving no stone unturned to stop ACTA, Polish Prime Minister Tusk committed his time and effort to persuade the Members of the EU Parliament (MEPs) who were in his European People's Party to vote against ACTA. The vote in Parliament would decide ACTA's fate.

Polish MEPs Rafał Trzaskowski, Róża Thun, and Paweł Zalewski, along with Igor Ostrowski, made the case against ACTA to other MEPs in Brussels. The massive street protests against ACTA had started to turn the tide in the EU Parliament. But many MEPs, including some from the EPP, were unfamiliar with the details of ACTA and still needed to be convinced to vote against it.

Paweł Zalewski was a member and vice chairman of the EU Parliament's Committee on International Trade (INTA), the key committee for ACTA's approval before the plenary vote. INTA usually was pro-IP enforcement, so it still might vote in favor of ACTA, notwithstanding all the protests. Zalewski, who had helped to run an underground press in defiance of the former Communist censorship regime in Poland during the 1980s, was especially concerned about Internet censorship. Like Prime Minister Tusk, who had been a journalist and a prominent student activist in Solidarity during the '80s, Zalewski had been shaped by his experience opposing the Communist regime.

"The '80s were a very formative time for me. I was in high school. I, together with about eighty colleagues, created the Pokolenie publishing house to oppose Communism, to oppose martial law," Zalewski explained.

"We started to publish books and information from underground Solidarity leadership. This freedom of expression, this freedom of thinking, this access to free ideas, we were able to win in 1989. I understood the power of culture, the power of free ideas, how important it was to the people."

Zalewski now made it his mission to convince other members of INTA to vote against ACTA. If INTA rejected ACTA, it would stand no chance of passing in the EU Parliament.

Internet nonprofits EDRi, Access Now, and the Trans Atlantic Consumer Dialogue published a short booklet on "What Makes ACTA So Controversial (and Why MEPs Should Care)" to educate the MEPs and the public about ACTA and its dangers to free speech and innovation.[28] The booklet was translated into 16 different languages of the EU countries. One-page fact sheets about ACTA were also distributed at the various street protests. Access Now organized an online petition against ACTA, which collected some 383,968 signatures, to send to MEPs.[29] Avaaz, the largest international group for online activists, secured over 2.8 million signatures with its own petition against ACTA.[30]

MEPs who were already against ACTA did their part to convince others to vote against ACTA. Led by Dutch MEP Marietje Schaake, touted by the *Wall Street Journal* as "Europe's Most Wired Politician,"[31] the Alliance of Democrats and Liberals for Europe (ALDE) held an important stakeholder hearing about ACTA in Parliament on April 11, 2012.[32] The room was packed, with sentiments strongly against ACTA. The problems with ACTA went well beyond the Internet chapter and included not only the secret manner in which it was negotiated outside of democratic processes, but also other provisions that could affect people's access to medicines.

By June 21, 2012, the debate in the EU Parliament turned against ACTA. INTA recommended rejecting ACTA by a 19–12 vote. Zalewski and his fellow Polish MEPs had helped to tip the balance in the INTA committee. Members and people in attendance applauded when the vote was revealed. The INTA vote followed earlier rejections that summer by four other EU Parliament committees: Civil Liberties, Development, Industry, and Legal Affairs. Without the support of INTA, ACTA was DOA.

On July 4, 2012, the EU Parliament convened in Strasbourg, France, to make it official. In a landslide vote of 478 against and only 39 in favor, the legislative body of the EU overwhelmingly rejected ACTA. The vote against ACTA was immediately projected on the big screen, which showed the exact breakdown of the votes by seats. The screen looked overwhelmingly red, which meant against ACTA. The electronic voting took only five minutes, but it was the most important vote for the EU Parliament and display of democracy for the EU since the Treaty of Lisbon had recognized greater legislative authority for the institution in 2009. Without the EU's involvement, ACTA was only a shell of the agreement the United States and other developed countries had sought.

After the historic vote in the EU Parliament, many MEPs applauded. MEPs from the Green Party, which played a huge part in the opposition to ACTA, even stood up from their seats in the EU Parliament holding up signs declaring: "Hello Democracy. Goodbye ACTA."

*   *   *

The historic vote against ACTA in the EU Parliament could not go without a celebration. The representatives from the various NGOs and volunteers who had fought so long and hard against ACTA convened later that afternoon at a local park. So did many MEPs and staffers who opposed ACTA. The party soon swelled to seventy people.

Jérémie Zimmermann, who had been working nonstop against ACTA for four years at La Quadrature du Net, quickly shifted from spokesperson to party organizer. He relished his new role.

"We popped twelve bottles of champagne, which we expensed without any shame," Zimmermann boasted gleefully.

The party lasted well into the night, shifting from the park to a local bar.

At 1 a.m., Zimmermann opened a special bottle of 1992 Dwojniak Kurpiowski Mead brought by a Polish volunteer who flew in for the July 4th ACTA vote. A traditional alcoholic beverage of Poland, the award-winning mead was made with nectar honey, plus blackcurrant juice. It was a special moment, given Poland's important role in igniting the mass protests against ACTA back in January 2012. Because there was only one bottle, Zimmermann carefully poured only a centiliter into each of fifty wine glasses so everyone could partake. The taste of victory was ever so sweet.

Raegan MacDonald, Access Now's senior policy analyst based in Belgium, summed it up best: "It was the celebration of all celebrations."

ACTA had consumed her life for over a year. Now it was suddenly over. She savored the moment. "It was something we thought was completely impossible. We were told by so many people that stopping ACTA would never happen. But it actually did."

Though ecstatic about the ACTA victory, MacDonald tried to temper her joy.

"We tried not to celebrate too much because it was just a battle. We won a battle, not the war. We're still fighting other free trade agreements and intellectual property enforcement that affect individual rights."

In a way, the fight for digital rights had only just begun.

Acknowledgments

A book cannot be written alone. I am indebted to the sixty-plus individuals who were involved in the historic events discussed herein and who agreed to be interviewed for this book. To a person, these individuals were ever so gracious with their time and ever so patient with my incessant questioning about the little details of the events. I know I tested not only their memories, but also their patience. I hope I have faithfully retold their stories.

I was fortunate to be invited to speak on a panel about SOPA with Alfred Perry, Vice President for Worldwide Content Protection & Outreach at Paramount Pictures, and Professor Irene Calboli of Marquette University Law School in April 2012. Though Paramount had supported SOPA (and lost), the movie studio should be commended for reaching out to students and law professors to learn more about why so many people opposed SOPA. The dialogue was incredibly productive and sealed my interest in telling this story.

My assistants Alison Steiner and Laura Caringella were a constant help throughout the entire process of writing this book, from proofreading and formatting to providing their substantive comments. They critiqued the first drafts, offering valuable feedback that helped me crystallize the organization of the book.

I had a team of students who were indispensable. James Baldwin was instrumental in getting this project off the ground by providing the preliminary research of SOPA. In meticulous detail,

Baldwin's research helped me to retrace the chronology of events all the way back to the beginning. Amy Harvey did the same in retracing the chronology of ACTA. Nadia Makki helped with further research. Michal Pekala, Dorota Kosela, Michal Rzadkowski, and Jessica Rzotkiewicz provided excellent translations and research of Polish sources. Sam Castree, III, along with Mary Katherine Schweihs, cite-checked all the sources. Castree, Makki, Rzotkiewicz, Benjamin Boroughf, Cole Garrett, Kenneth Matuszewski, Millie Parkara, Sara Smith, Rebecca Sundin, Laurence Tooth, and my former student Kristi Wilcox helped with the final round of proofreading and critiquing the book.

My law school IIT Chicago-Kent College of Law has provided unflagging support for all of my research. I wrote most of the book while on sabbatical in fall 2012 under a research grant from the law school and with support from the Norman and Edna Freehling Scholars program. Dean Hal Krent backed the book from the start—not to mention, he's a fellow devoted Cleveland sports fan.

Tom Gaylord, Chicago-Kent research librarian, tracked down many sources related to my research for this book and my other writings on the freedom of the Internet. John Young and Gwendolyn Osborne of our Public Affairs office helped promote the book, as did our social media strategist Allison Bernstein and webmaster Michael Miller. Daniel Saunders did an incredible job formatting the book for print copies.

My agent, Carol Mann, believed this story needed to be told.

My illustrator, Cortney Skinner, took my vision and turned it into a piece of art. I could not imagine a cover that could better represent this book—or the free Internet movement. Collaborating with Cortney was a sheer joy.

Friends and colleagues reviewed drafts of my book proposal or the book itself, or gave much needed moral support in my periods of self-doubt: Julie Aquino, Andy Beights, David Caplan, Isabella Chow, Carl Dechiara, Katheryn Ellis, Jaime Hamrick, Angela Hennies, Robert Jeng, Bob Kim, Andrew Klausmeyer, Jennifer Levin, Erin Lothson, Mamta Mujumdar, Stephani Ramirez, Jake

Saxbe, Chris Schmidt, Amethyst Smith, Peter Taylor, and Kristi Wilcox. Their advice, enthusiasm, and support were invaluable. And my closest friends endured either far too many stories about SOPA from me or long periods of silence when I basically went off the grid while writing this book. Their indulgence was ever so kind. I'm lucky to have them as friends.

Dan and Parmalee Thatcher were generous to let me write this book at their lovely place in Sausalito, which was a great source of inspiration.

My parents, Douglas and Catalina Lee, sacrificed more for me than I can possibly fathom or ever repay. Their love and support are never-ending. Kathy and Rich are the best siblings a person can ask for. I wouldn't be who I am without them.

Notes

Most of the quotes from outside sources are indicated in the notes above. Consecutive quotes from the same source were noted by only one citation. Some quotes that are in the public record of Congress were not cited at all, given the ease of finding them in the public record. Most quotes that have no citations and that are not in the public record were based on interviews I conducted with over 60 individuals.

Introduction

[1] THE POETICAL WORKS OF HENRY WADSWORTH LONGFELLOW 238, 240 (1879).

[2] DAVID HACKETT FISCHER, PAUL REVERE'S RIDE 138 (1994).

[3] *Id.* at 79.

[4] *Id.* at 139.

[5] *Id.* at 79.

[6] WIKIPEDIA, http://en.wikipedia.org/?banner=blackout.

[7] *See* Timothy B. Lee, *PIPA Support Collapses, with 13 New Senators Opposed,* ARS TECHNICA, Jan. 18, 2012, http://arstechnica.com/tech-policy/2012/01/pipa-support-collapses-with-13-new-opponents-in-senate/; Declan McCullagh & Elinor Mills, *Protests Lead to Weakening Support for Protect IP, SOPA,* CNET, Jan. 18, 2012, http://news.cnet.com/8301-31921_3-57361237-281/protests-lead-to-weakening-support-for-protect-ip-sopa/.

[8] *See Hollywood vs. Silicon Valley*, NBC LOS ANGELES, Feb. 16, 2012, http://www.nbclosangeles.com/blogs/prop-zero/Hollywood-vs-Silicon-Valley-137920383.html; Julia Boorstin, *Anti-Piracy Bill Battle: Hollywood v. Silicon Valley,* CNBC, Dec. 8, 2011, http://www.cnbc.com/id/45605252.

⁹ Viveca Novak, *SOPA and PIPA Spur Lobbying Spike*, OPENSECRETS, Jan. 26, 2012, http://www.opensecrets.org/news/2012/01/sopa-and-pipa-create-lobbying-spike.html.

¹⁰ *F2C2012: Aaron Swartz Keynote: "How We Stopped SOPA,"* YOUTUBE, May 22, 2012, http://youtu.be/Fgh2dFngFsg?t=21m26s.

¹¹ FISCHER, *supra* note 2, at 138.

Chapter 1: Free Bieber

¹ PROTECT IP Act (PIPA), S. 968, *available at* http://www.gpo.gov/fdsys/pkg/BILLS-112s968is/pdf/BILLS-112s968is.pdf.

² Commercial Felony Streaming Act, S. 978, *available at* http://www.gpo.gov/fdsys/pkg/BILLS-112s978is/pdf/BILLS-112s978is.pdf.

³ PIPA, § 3, S. 968, *supra* note 12.

⁴ Charlie Savage & Leslie Kaufman, *Phone Records of Journalists Seized by U.S.*, N.Y. TIMES, May 13, 2013, at A1; Charlie Savage & Jonathan Weisman, *Holder Faces New Round of Criticism After Leak Inquiries*, N.Y. TIMES, May 29, 2013, at A16.

⁵ PIPA, § 4, S. 968, *supra* note 12.

⁶ Combating Online Infringement and Counterfeits Act (COICA), S. 3804, *available at* http://www.gpo.gov/fdsys/pkg/BILLS-111s3804is/pdf/BILLS-111s3804is.pdf.

⁷ Steve Crocker *et al.*, White Paper, *Security and Other Technical Concerns Raised by the DNS Filtering Requirements in the PROTECT IP Bill*, May 2011, http://s3.amazonaws.com/dmk/PROTECT-IP-Technical-Whitepaper-Final.pdf.

⁸ Peter Eckersley, *An Open Letter from Internet Engineers to the Senate Judiciary Committee*, DEEP LINKS (blog), Electronic Frontier Foundation, Sept. 28, 2010, https://www.eff.org/deeplinks/2010/09/open-letter.

⁹ Institute for Policy Innovation, *The True Cost of Copyright Industry Piracy to the U.S. Economy*, Oct. 2007, at i, http://www.ipi.org/docLib/20120515_Copyright-Piracy.pdf.

¹⁰ Government Accountability Office, *Intellectual Property: Observations on Efforts to Quantify the Economic Effects of Counterfeit and Pirated Goods*, GAO-10-423, at 15-19 (2008), http://www.gao.gov/new.items/d10423.pdf.

¹¹ Joe Karagis, The American Assembly Columbia University, *Where Do Music Collections Come From?*, Oct. 15, 2012, http://piracy.americanassembly.org/where-do-music-collections-come-from/.

¹² Julian Sanchez, *How Copyright Industries Con Congress*, CATO AT LIBERTY (blog), Jan. 3, 2012, http://www.cato.org/blog/how-copyright-industries-con-congress.

¹³ Keith Peters, *Jeremy Lin Proving That He's the Real NBA Deal*, PALO ALTO ONLINE, Feb. 16, 2012, http://www.paloaltoonline.com/news/show_story.php?id=24350.

¹⁴ PIPA, Bill Summary, Sponsors, http://thomas.loc.gov/cgi-bin/bdquery/z?d112:SN00968:@@@P.

¹⁵ Stop Online Piracy Act (SOPA), § 103, H.R. 3261, *available at* http://thomas.loc.gov/home/gpoxmlc112/h3261_ih.xml (emphasis added).

¹⁶ Complaint at ¶ 76, Viacom Int'l Inc. v. YouTube, Inc., 718 F. Supp. 2d 514 (S.D.N.Y. 2010) (No. 1:07-cv-02103-LLS) (filed March 13, 2007) (emphasis added), *available at* http://online.wsj.com/public/resources/documents/Viacom031207.pdf.

¹⁷ Prioritizing Resources and Organization for Intellectual Property Act of 2008, Pub. L. No. 110-403, § 206, 122 Stat. 4256 (2008); 18 U.S.C. § 2323.

¹⁸ Tia Ghose, *'This Domain Has Been Seized by ICE,'* CENTER FOR INVESTIGATIVE REPORTING, Dec. 3, 2010, http://cironline.org/blog/post/domain-has-been-seized-ice-858.

¹⁹ Nate Anderson, *Government Admits Defeat, Gives Back Rojadirecta Domains*, ARS TECHNICA, Aug. 29, 2012, http://arstechnica.com/tech-policy/2012/08/government-goes-0-2-admits-defeat-in-rojadirecta-domain-forfeit-case/.

²⁰ Ted Samson, *Feds Wrongly Links 84,000 Seized Sites to Child Porn*, PC WORLD, Feb. 18, 2011, http://www.pcworld.com/article/220113/feds_wrongly_link_8400_seized_sites_to_child_porn.html.

²¹ *McCartney Is Down with Hip-Hop*, 103 WODS FM, Feb. 24, 2011, http://cbswods2.wordpress.com/2011/02/24/paul-mccartney-is-down-with-hip-hop/.

²² *Jay-Z: The Fresh Air Interview*, NPR, Nov. 16, 2010, http://www.npr.org/2010/11/16/131334322/the-fresh-air-interview-jay-z-decoded?ft=1&f=13.

²³ Bridgeport Music, Inc. v. Dimension Films, 410 F.3d 792, 801 (6th Cir. 2005).

²⁴ Commercial Felony Streaming Act, § 1(a)(1)(B), S. 978, *available at* http://www.gpo.gov/fdsys/pkg/BILLS-112s978is/pdf/BILLS-112s978is.pdf.

²⁵ Victoria Espinel, *Concrete Steps Congress Can Take to Protect America's Intellectual Property*, THE WHITE HOUSE BLOG, March 15, 2011, http://www.whitehouse.gov/blog/2011/03/15/concrete-steps-congress-can-take-protect-americas-intellectual-property; Obama Administration's White Paper on Intellectual Property Enforcement Legislative Recommendations, March 2011, at 2, http://www.whitehouse.gov/sites/default/files/ip_white_paper.pdf.

²⁶ 17 U.S.C. § 506.

²⁷ Kidrauhl, *With You, Chris Brown Cover, Justin Singing*, YOUTUBE, Feb. 10, 2008, http://youtu.be/eQOFRZ1wNLw.

²⁸ Kidrauhl, YOUTUBE, http://www.youtube.com/user/kidrauhl/videos?flow=grid&view=0&sort=da.

²⁹ Matt Miller, *Amp Up the Sync*, THE DEAL PIPELINE, Feb. 22, 2013, http://www.thedeal.com/content/tmt/amp-up-the-sync.php.

³⁰ SOPA § 201, *supra* note 26.

³¹ David Taintor, *Does the Commercial Felony Streaming Act Threaten Internet Freedom*, TPM, Nov. 2, 2011, http://tpmdc.talkingpointsmemo.com/2011/11/does-a-senate-bill-threaten-internet-freedom.php.

³² Sony BMG Music Entm't v. Tenenbaum, 660 F.3d 487, 507-08 (1st Cir. 2011).

³³ Capitol Records, Inc. v. Thomas-Rasset, 692 F.3d 899, 908-10 (8th Cir. 2012); Sony BMG Music Entm't v. Tenenbaum, 660 F.3d 487 (1st Cir. 2011).

³⁴ Lizzie Widdicombe, *Teen Titan: The Man Who Made Justin Bieber*, THE NEW YORKER, Sept. 3, 2012, at 54.

³⁵ Jonathan Zittrain *et al.*, *A Close Look at SOPA*, Dec. 2, 2011, http://futureoftheinternet.org/reading-sopa.

[36] Sxephil, *S.978 + Melanie Iglesias Slootpacalypse 2011*, YouTube, Oct. 24, 2011, http://youtu.be/NpMptgTS7QQ?t=3m54s.

[37] Fight for the Future, *PROTECT IP / SOPA Breaks the Internet*, http://www.fightforthefuture.org/pipa/.

[38] Elizabeth Frock, *Could S. 978 Land Artists Like Bieber in Jail?*, WorldViews Blog, Wash. Post, October 25, 2011, http://www.washingtonpost.com/blogs/blogpost/post/s978-commercial-felony-streaming-act-could-it-land-artists-like-justin-bieber-in-jail/2011/10/25/gIQAnkfgFM_blog.html.

[39] *Bieber Is Right*, http://www.bieberisright.org (audio of interview).

[40] *Justin Bieber: Klobuchar Should Be "Locked Up,"* Minn. Star Tribune, Oct. 28, 2011, http://www.startribune.com/politics/statelocal/132782298.html.

[41] *Justin Bieber in Verbal Dispute with Amy Klobuchar*, CBS Minnesota, Oct. 28, 2011, http://minnesota.cbslocal.com/2011/10/28/justin-bieber-in-verbal-dispute-with-amy-klobuchar/.

[42] Catalina Camia, *Justin Bieber: Sen. Klobuchar Should Be Jailed*, USA Today, Oct. 28, 2011, http://content.usatoday.com/communities/onpolitics/post/2011/10/justin-bieber-amy-klobuchar-streaming-content-/1#.T-HTvWjF_ww; Aaron Rasmussen, *Justin Bieber: Sen. Amy Klobuchar Should 'Be Locked Up' for Supporting Felony Streaming Act*, N.Y. Daily News, Nov. 1, 2011, http://articles.nydailynews.com/2011-11-01/news/30347891_1_justin-bieber-youtube-channel-amy-klobuchar.

[43] David Henry, *Justin Bieber Says Amy Klobuchar Should Be 'Locked Up,'* Minn. Post, Oct. 28, 2011, http://www.minnpost.com/dc-dispatches/2011/10/justin-bieber-says-amy-klobuchar-should-be-locked

[44] *Music Speaks Up on Erroneous Web Campaign*, Copyright Alliance, Oct. 29, 2011, http://blog.copyrightalliance.org/2011/10/music-speaks-up-on-erroneous-web-campaign/.

[45] SOPA, Bill Summary, Cosponsors, http://thomas.loc.gov/cgi-bin/bdquery/z?d112:HR03261:@@@P.

Chapter 2: American Censorship Day

[1] Declan McCullagh, *Vint Cerf: SOPA Means 'Unprecedented Censorship' of the Web*, CNET, Dec. 15, 2011, http://news.cnet.com/8301-31921_3-57344028-281/vint-cerf-sopa-means-unprecedented-censorship-of-the-web/.

[2] *See* Malcolm Gladwell, The Tipping Point: How Little Things Can Make a Big Difference 30 (2002).

[3] Harvey Anderson, HJA's Blog, Dec. 9, 2011, http://lockshot.wordpress.com/2011/11/09/sopa-the-stop-online-piracy-act-is-it-really-dangerous/.

[4] Declan McCullagh, *Google, Facebook, Zynga Oppose New SOPA Copyright Bill*, CNET, Nov. 15, 2011, http://news.cnet.com/8301-31921_3-57325134-281/google-facebook-zynga-oppose-new-sopa-copyright-bill/.

[5] Rebecca MacKinnon, *Stop the Great Firewall of America*, N.Y. Times, Nov. 15, 2011, http://www.nytimes.com/2011/11/16/opinion/firewall-law-could-infringe-on-free-speech.html.

[6] An Open Letter to House of Representatives submitted by Profs. Mark

Lemley, David Levine, and David Post on behalf of 110 Law Professors, Nov. 15, 2011, *available at* https://www.cdt.org/files/pdfs/SOPA_House_letter_with_PROTECT_IP_letter_FINAL.pdf.

[7] Letter to Chairman Smith and Ranking Member Conyers from Human Rights and Internet Rights Organizations, Nov. 15, 2011, https://www.laquadrature.net/files/SOPA_Letter_to_HR.pdf.

[8] Mike Masnick, *The Secret Behind SOPA Defense: Insist That It Doesn't Say What It Actually Says*, TECHDIRT, Nov. 7, 2011, http://www.techdirt.com/articles/20111104/23411816644/secret-behind-sopa-defense-insist-that-it-doesnt-say-what-it-actually-says.shtml.

[9] Damien Scott, *Tumblr Fights Against the Stop Online Piracy Act with Censorship Scare*, COMPLEXTECH, Nov. 16, 2011, http://www.complex.com/tech/2011/11/tumblr-fights-against-the-stop-online-piracy-act-with-censorship-scare.

[10] Tumblr Staff Feed, TUMBLR, Nov. 17, 2011, http://staff.tumblr.com/post/12930076128/a-historic-thing.

[11] Interview with David Karp, *Can Tumblr Stop SOPA?*, YouTube, Nov. 22, 2011, http://youtu.be/FPfKwyWOpzA?t=30s.

[12] House Judiciary Committee, Hearing on H.R.3261, the "Stop Online Piracy Act," Nov. 16, 2011, http://judiciary.house.gov/hearings/printers/112th/112-154_71240.PDF [SOPA Hearing].

[13] National Association of Boards of Pharmacy, *Counterfeit Drugs*, http://www.nabp.net/programs/consumer-protection/buying-medicine-online/counterfeit-drugs.

[14] Alicia Mundy, *Measure to Allow Drug Imports Fails*, WALL ST. J., Dec. 16, 2009, http://online.wsj.com/article/SB126093494955393151.html.

[15] Department of Justice, Press Release, *Google Forfeits $500 Million Generated by Online Ads & Prescription Drug Sales by Canadian Online Pharmacies*, Aug. 24, 2011, http://www.justice.gov/opa/pr/2011/August/11-dag-1078.html.

[16] Stewart Baker, *Finding Fault with the Stop Online Piracy Act*, SKATING ON STILTS (blog), Nov. 18, 2011, http://www.skatingonstilts.com/skating-on-stilts/2011/11/finding-fault-with-the-stop-online-piracy-act.html.

[17] SOPA Hearing, *supra* note 68, at 255-57.

[18] Eshoo Letter to Chairman Smith and Ranking Member Conyers, Nov. 15, 2011, http://eshoo.house.gov/index.php?option=com_content&view=article&id=1107.

[19] SOPA Strike Timeline, http://sopastrike.com/timeline (entry for November 16, 2011).

[20] Nancy Pelosi, TWITTER, Nov. 17, 2011, https://twitter.com/NancyPelosi/status/137234283667537920.

[21] EU Parliament, Joint Motion for a Resolution on the EU-US Summit of 28 November 2011, Nov. 17, 2011, http://www.europarl.europa.eu/sides/getDoc.do?type=MOTION&reference=P7-RC-2011-0577&language=EN.

Chapter 3: Bring in the Nerds

[1] Editorial, *Piracy vs. an Open Internet*, L.A. TIMES, Nov. 25, 2011, http://articles.latimes.com/2011/nov/25/opinion/la-ed-newpiracy-20111125; Editorial, *Going*

After Pirates, N.Y. Times, Nov. 26, 2011, http://www.nytimes.com/2011/11/27/opinion/sunday/going-after-the-pirates.html.

² *Stop Online Piracy Act – Danny Goldberg & Jonathan Zittrain*, The Colbert Report, Dec. 1, 2011, http://www.colbertnation.com/the-colbert-report-videos/403466/december-01-2011/stop-online-piracy-act---danny-goldberg---jonathan-zittrain.

³ Rachel Weiner, *The White House Pushed Dirt on Darrell Issa, Book Says*, Post Politics (blog), Wash. Post, July 3, 2013, http://www.washingtonpost.com/blogs/post-politics/wp/2013/07/03/the-white-house-pushed-dirt-on-darrell-issa-book-says/.

⁴ Ezra Klein, *Sen. Wyden: Romney's Plan Hurts the 'Poorest and Most Vulnerable Seniors,"* Wash. Post, Aug. 14, 2012, http://www.washingtonpost.com/blogs/wonkblog/wp/2012/08/14/sen-wyden-romneys-plan-hurts-the-poorest-and-most-vulnerable-seniors/.

⁵ Julian Pecquet, *Bipartisan Bill Would Accelerate State Opt-out Provision in Health Law*, The Hill, Nov. 22, 1010, http://thehill.com/blogs/healthwatch/health-reform-implementation/130295-bipartisan-bill-would-accelerate-state-op-out-provision-in-healthcare-law.

⁶ Sam Baker, *Wyden Calls for Changes in Key ObamaCare Program*, June 13, 2013, http://thehill.com/blogs/healthwatch/medicare/305423-wyden-calls-for-changes-in-key-obamacare-program.

⁷ Keep the Web Open, OPEN: Online Protection & Enforcement of Digital Trade Act, *available at* http://www.keepthewebopen.com/open ["OPEN Act"].

⁸ *Id.* § 2(f)(2)(C).

⁹ Laurence H. Tribe, *The "Stop Online Piracy Act" (SOPA) Violates the First Amendment*, http://www.scribd.com/doc/75153093/Tribe-Legis-Memo-on-SOPA-12-6-11-1.

¹⁰ Letter by Floyd Abrams to Chairman Lamar Smith re SOPA, Nov. 7, 20111, http://www.mpaa.org/resources/1227ef12-e209-4edf-b8b8-bb4af768430c.pdf.

¹¹ Letter by Marvin Ammori to U.S. Congress re: PROTECT IP Act and Stop Online Privacy Act, Dec. 8, 2011, http://ammori.files.wordpress.com/2011/12/ammori-first-amd-sopa-protectip.pdf.

¹² Amendment in the Nature of a Substitute to H.R. 3261 Offered by Mr. Smith of Texas, § 103(b), http://judiciary.house.gov/hearings/pdf/HR%203261%20Managers%20Amendment.pdf ["SOPA Manager's Amendment"]; Statement from Chairman Smith on Senate Delay of Vote on PROTECT IP Act, http://judiciary.house.gov/issues/issues_RogueWebsites.html.

¹³ SOPA Manager's Amendment §§ 101(23) (definition of U.S. directed site), 103(a)(1)(A)(ii), *supra* note 89.

¹⁴ *Id.* § 102(c)(2)(A).

¹⁵ *Id.* § 102(c)(2)(A)(ii).

¹⁶ House Judiciary Committee, Full Committee Markup of H.R. 3261, Transcript 264-65 (Dec. 15, 2011) (Lofgren statement).

¹⁷ SOPA Manager's Amendment, § 2(a)(A), *supra* note 89.

¹⁸ *See, e.g., Congressman Mel Watt Defends SOPA (Stop Online Piracy Act),* Dec. 16, 2011, http://youtu.be/i6x1sYYqKLY.

¹⁹ Alexandra Petri, *The Nightmarish SOPA Hearings*, ComPost (blog),

WASH. POST, Dec. 15, http://www.washingtonpost.com/blogs/compost/post/the-nightmarish-sopa-hearings/2011/12/15/gIQA47RUwO_blog.html.

[20] Perez Hilton, *Jon Stewart vs. SOPA Sponsors*, Jan. 19, 2012, http://perezhilton.com/2012-01-19-jon-stewart-takes-on-sopa-sponsors-in-highlarious-clips-from-the-daily-show#.UHbRr0LF_wx.

[21] Letter to Rep. Zoe Lofgren from Dr. Leonard Napolitano, Jr., Nov. 16, 2011, http://www.scribd.com/doc/73106069/Napolitano-Response-Rep-Lofgren-11-16-11-c.

[22] An Open Letter from Internet Engineers to the United States Congress, Dec. 15, 2011, https://www.eff.org/sites/default/files/Internet-Engineers-Letter.pdf.

[23] Daniel Castro, Richard Bennett & Scott Andes, ITIF, *Steal These Policies: Strategies for Reducing Digital Piracy*, Dec. 15, 2009, http://archive.itif.org/index.php?id=324.

[24] Daniel Castro, *PIPA/SOPA: Responding to Critics and Finding a Path Forward*, Dec. 2011, at 9-10, http://www.itif.org/files/2011-pipa-sopa-respond-critics.pdf.

[25] Mike Masnick, *MPAA Joins RIAA in Having Budgets Slashed*, TECHDIRT, Aug. 27, 2012, http://www.techdirt.com/articles/20120827/02295920166/mpaa-joins-riaa-having-budgets-slashed.shtml.

[26] Google, *U.S. Public Policy: Transparency*, http://www.google.com/publicpolicy/transparency.html.

[27] Letter to Leahy, Grassley, Smith, Conyers from Steve Crocker *et al.*, Dec. 9, 2011, at 2, http://www.circleid.com/pdf/letter-to-us-hr-regarding-sopa.pdf.

[28] Self-Prodigy, *GoDaddy Supports SOPA, I'm Transferring 51 Domains & Suggesting a Move Your Domain Day*, REDDIT, Dec. 22, 2011, http://www.reddit.com/r/politics/comments/nmnie/godaddy_supports_sopa_im_transferring_51_domains/?limit=500.

[29] Ben Huh, TWITTER, Dec. 22, 2011, https://twitter.com/benhuh/status/149965881479397376.

[30] Thea Chard, *Cheezburger CEO Ben Huh on Surrounding Himself with More Talent, and the Future of the Global Humor Blog Network*, XCONOMY, June 30, 2010, http://www.xconomy.com/seattle/2010/06/30/cheezburger-ceo-ben-huh-on-surrounding-himself-with-more-talent-and-the-future-of-the-global-humor-blog-network/.

[31] Timothy B. Lee, *GoDaddy Faces Boycott Over SOPA Support*, ARS TECHNICA, Dec. 22, 2011, http://arstechnica.com/tech-policy/2011/12/godaddy-faces-december-29-boycott-over-sopa-support/.

[32] Timothy B. Lee, *Victory! Boycott Forces GoDaddy to Drop Its Support for SOPA*, ARS TECHNICA, Dec. 23, 2011, http://arstechnica.com/tech-policy/2011/12/victory-boycott-forces-godaddy-to-drop-its-support-for-sopa/.

[33] Tom Chereder, *Go Daddy Loses Over 37,000 Domains Due to SOPA Stance*, VENTURE BEAT, Dec. 24, 2011, http://venturebeat.com/2011/12/24/godaddy-domain-loss/; Declan McCullagh, *GoDaddy Accused of Interfering with Anti-SOPA Exodus*, CNET, Dec. 26, 2011, http://news.cnet.com/8301-31921_3-57348511-281/godaddy-accused-of-interfering-with-anti-sopa-exodus/.

[34] Agatha Christie, *The Last Séance* in THE HOUND OF DEATH 218 (1933).

[35] *Stop the E-Parasite Act*, Petition, WE THE PEOPLE, THE WHITE HOUSE,

Oct. 31, 2011, https://petitions.whitehouse.gov/petition/stop-e-parasite-act/ SWBYXX55.

[36] *VETO the SOPA Bill and Any Other Future Bills that Threaten to Diminish the Free Flow of Information*, Petition, We the People, The White House, Dec. 18, 2011, https://wwws.whitehouse.gov/petitions/%252F!/petition/veto-sopa-bill-and-any-other-future-bills-threaten-diminish-free-flow-information/g3W1BscR.

[37] Brendan Sasso, *White House to Respond to Petition Urging Veto of Online Piracy Bill*, The Hill, Dec. 22, 2011, http://thehill.com/blogs/hillicon-valley/technology/200975-white-house-to-respond-to-petition-urging-veto-of-anti-piracy-bill.

[38] Brendan Sasso, *GOP Chairman Expects Obama to Sign Anti-Online Piracy Bill*, The Hill, Dec. 18, 2011, http://thehill.com/blogs/hillicon-valley/technology/200133-gop-chairman-expects-obama-to-sign-anti-piracy-bill.

[39] Lachlan Markay, *Senate Conservatives Warn Reid Against PROTECT IP Blitz*, Heritage, Jan. 13, 2012, http://blog.heritage.org/2012/01/13/senate-conservatives-warn-reid-against-protect-ip-blitz/.

[40] Victoria Espinel, Aneesh Chopra & Howard Schmidt, *Combating Online Piracy While Protecting an Open and Innovative Internet*, The White House, Jan. 17, 2012, http://www.whitehouse.gov/blog/2012/01/14/obama-administration-responds-we-people-petitions-sopa-and-online-piracy.

Chapter 4: Wikipedia Blackout

[1] *Issa Statement on #SOPA & #PIPA Website Blackouts*, Jan. 18, 2012, http://oversight.house.gov/release/issa-statement-on-sopa-pipa-website-blackouts/.

[2] Jennifer Van Grove, *Google and Facebook Reign as the Most-Visited Sites of 2011*, Venture Beat, Dec. 28, 2011, http://venturebeat.com/2011/12/28/google-top-web-brand/.

[3] User Talk: Jimbo Wales/Archive 91, *Request for Comment: SOPA and a Strike*, Dec. 10, 2011, https://en.wikipedia.org/wiki/User_talk:Jimbo_Wales/Archive_91.

[4] User Talk: Jimbo Wales/Archive 91, *Request for Comment: SOPA and a Strike*, Dec. 10, 2011, https://en.wikipedia.org/wiki/User_talk:Jimbo_Wales/Archive_91#Result.

[5] Village Pump, *Participation in Anti-SOPA and Anti-PIPA Protests by Blacking Out the Wikipedia Logo for One Day (Tomorrow, Nov. 16)*, http://en.wikipedia.org/wiki/Wikipedia:Village_pump_%28proposals%29/Archive_80#Participation_in_anti-SOPA_and_anti-PIPA_protests_by_blacking_out_the_Wikipedia_logo_for_one_day_.28TOMORROW.2C_NOV._16th.29.

[6] Wikipedia, *SOPA Initiative/Action, Call for Comment from the Community*, Jan. 13, 2012, http://en.wikipedia.org/wiki/Wikipedia:SOPA_initiative/Action#Call_for_comment_from_the_community.

[7] Wikipedia, SOPA Initiative/Action, http://en.wikipedia.org/wiki/Wikipedia:SOPA_initiative/Action.

[8] Jimmy Wales, Twitter, Jan. 16, 2012, https://twitter.com/jimmy_wales/status/158971314449809409.

[9] Sue Gardner, *Wikipedia's Community Calls for Anti-SOPA Blackout January*

18, Jan. 16, 2012, http://blog.wikimedia.org/2012/01/16/wikipedias-community-calls-for-anti-sopa-blackout-january-18/.

¹⁰ Wikipedia, *SOPA initiative/Learn More,* https://en.wikipedia.org/w/index.php?title=Wikipedia:SOPA_initiative/Learn_more&oldid=471995984.

¹¹ *Wikimedia Foundation SOPA War Room Meeting 1-17-2012-1-9,* http://commons.wikimedia.org/wiki/File:Wikimedia_Foundation_SOPA_War_Room_Meeting_1-17-2012-1-9.jpg; http://commons.wikimedia.org/wiki/File:Wikimedia_Foundation_SOPA_War_Room_Meeting_1-17-2012-1-7.jpg.

¹² Wikipedia, http://en.wikipedia.org/?banner=blackout.

¹³ *Video of Wikimedia Foundation Wikipedia Blackout SOPA January 18, 2012,* https://commons.wikimedia.org/wiki/File:Wikimedia_Foundation_Wikipedia_Blackout_SOPA_January_18,_2012.theora.ogv.

¹⁴ Declan McCullagh & Greg Sandoval, *Google Will Protest SOPA Using Popular Home Page,* CNET, Jan. 17, 2012, http://news.cnet.com/8301-31001_3-57360223-261/google-will-protest-sopa-using-popular-home-page/.

¹⁵ Devin Coldewey, *Eric Schmidt Doubles Down on SOPA Bill, Describing It as "Censorship," "Draconian,"* TechCrunch, Nov. 15, 2011, http://techcrunch.com/2011/11/15/eric-schmidt-doubles-down-on-sopa-bill-describing-it-as-censorship-draconian/.

¹⁶ Ned Potter, *SOPA Blackout: Wikipedia, Google, Wired Protest 'Internet Censorship,'* ABC News, Jan. 18, 2012, http://abcnews.go.com/blogs/technology/2012/01/sopa-blackout-wikipedia-google-wired-join-protest-against-internet-censorship/.

¹⁷ *SOPA Sponsor Calls Protests a 'Publicity Stunt' as Google Joins Up,* PC Mag., Jan. 17, 2012, http://www.pcmag.com/article2/0,2817,2398985,00.asp.

¹⁸ SOPA Strike Timeline, http://sopastrike.com/timeline (entry for Jan. 18, 2012).

¹⁹ Anthony Ha, *Mark Zuckerberg Posts Against SOPA, Suddenly Remembers Twitter Account,* TechCrunch, Jan. 18, 2012, http://techcrunch.com/2012/01/18/mark-zuckerberg-sopa-pipa/.

²⁰ Wikipedia, *SOPA Initiative/Learn More,* http://en.wikipedia.org/wiki/Wikipedia:SOPA_initiative/Learn_more.

²¹ Declan McCullagh, *Protect IP, SOPA Protests Knock Senate Web Sites Offline,* CNET, Jan. 18, 2012, http://news.cnet.com/8301-31921_3-57361322-281/protect-ip-sopa-protests-knock-senate-web-sites-offline/.

²² Khan Academy, *SOPA and PIPA: What SOPA and PIPA Are at Face Value and What They Could End Up Enabling,* Jan. 18, 2012, http://www.khanacademy.org/humanities/american-civics/v/sopa-and-pipa.

²³ Khan Academy, *SOPA and PIPA,* http://www.youtube.com/watch?v=tzqMoOk9NWc.

²⁴ Google, *End Piracy, Not Liberty,* Jan. 18, 2012, https://www.google.com/takeaction/past-actions/end-piracy-not-liberty/index.html; *SOPA Strike Numbers,* http://sopastrike.com/numbers/.

²⁵ *SOPA Strike Numbers, supra* note 141.

²⁶ McCullagh, *supra* note 138.

²⁷ *SOPA Strike Numbers, supra* note 141; Stan Schroeder, *SOPA Explodes on Twitter, Generates 2.4 Million Tweets,* Mashable, Jan. 19, 2012, http://mashable.

com/2012/01/19/sopa-tweets/.

[28] Ashton Kutcher, TWITTER, Jan. 19, 2012, http://twitter.com/aplusk/status/159717994166095872.

[29] Tina Korbe, *Even Ashton Kutcher Dislikes SOPA*, HOT AIR, Dec. 22, 2011, http://hotair.com/archives/2011/12/22/even-ashton-kutcher-dislikes-sopa/.

[30] Karin Tanabe, *Issa Tweets Ashton Kutcher Over SOPA*, POLITICO, Dec. 22, 2011, http://www.politico.com/blogs/click/2011/12/issa-tweets-ashton-kutcher-over-sopa-108511.html.

[31] Kim Kardashian, TWITTER, Jan. 18, 2012, http://twitter.com/KimKardashian/status/159819209206022144.

[32] *Growing Chorus of Opposition to "Stop Online Piracy Act,"* https://www.cdt.org/report/growing-chorus-opposition-stop-online-piracy-act; *List of Those Expressing Concern with SOPA & PIPA*, https://www.cdt.org/report/list-organizations-and-individuals-opposing-sopa.

[33] Jenna Wortham, *Protests Against Antipiracy Bills to Take to Streets*, BITS (blog), N.Y. TIMES, Jan. 18, 2012, http://bits.blogs.nytimes.com/2012/01/18/techies-plan-to-take-sopa-protest-to-the-streets/?smid=pl-share.

[34] *MC Hammer Speaks Out Against SOPA*, YouTube, Jan. 18, 2012, http://www.youtube.com/watch?v=lX1cDL17R0E.

[35] Timothy B. Lee, *PIPA Support Collapses, with 13 New Senators Opposed*, ARS TECHNICA, Jan. 18, 2012, http://arstechnica.com/tech-policy/2012/01/pipa-support-collapses-with-13-new-opponents-in-senate/.

[36] James L. Gattuso, *Online Piracy and SOPA: Beware of Unintended Consequences*, THE HERITAGE FOUNDATION, Dec. 21, 2011, http://www.heritage.org/research/reports/2011/12/online-piracy-and-sopa-beware-of-unintended-consequences/.

[37] Erick Erickson, *Stopping SOPA*, REDSTATE, Dec. 22, 2011, http://www.redstate.com/erick/2011/12/22/stopping-sopa/.

[38] Sen. Marco Rubio, *A Better Way to Fight the Online Theft of American Ideas and Jobs*, FACEBOOK, Jan. 18, 2012, http://www.facebook.com/SenatorMarcoRubio/posts/340889625936408.

[39] Roger Yu, *SOPA Protest Gets Intended Effect*, USA TODAY, Jan. 18, 2012, http://www.usatoday.com/tech/news/story/2012-01-18/SOPA-PIPA-protest-reaction/52641560/1.

[40] Josh Constine, *SOPA Protests Sway Congress: 31 Opponents Yesterday, 122 Now*, TECHCRUNCH, Jan. 19, 2012, http://techcrunch.com/2012/01/19/sopa-opponents-supporters/.

[41] Newt Gingrich, *Newt Slams SOPA*, YouTube, Jan. 19, 2012, http://www.youtube.com/watch?v=CDbSWZpHBog.

[42] *Republican Candidates Oppose SOPA*, YouTube, Jan. 20, 2012, http://youtu.be/LOoYgwbVca4.

[43] Stewart Baker, *The SOPA War: Why the GOP Turned on Piracy*, HOLLYWOOD REPORTER, Feb. 2, 2012, http://www.hollywoodreporter.com/news/sopa-hollywood-gop-piracy-286648.

[44] Statement from Chairman Smith on Senate Delay of Vote on PROTECT IP Act, House Judiciary Comm., Jan. 20, 2012, http://judiciary.house.gov/issues/issues_RogueWebsites.html.

⁴⁵ Comment of Senator Patrick Leahy on Postponement of the Vote on Cloture on the Motion to Proceed to the PROTECT IP Act, Jan. 20, 2012, http://www.leahy.senate.gov/press/comment-of-senator-patrick-leahy-on-postponement-of-the-vote-on-cloture-on-the-motion-to-proceed-to-the-protect-ip-act.

⁴⁶ Sue Gardner, *The Message from the Wikipedia Blackout: Please Leave the Internet Alone*, WIKIMEDIA BLOG, Jan. 20, 2012, http://blog.wikimedia.org/2012/01/20/the-message-from-the-wikipedia-blackout-please-leave-the-internet-alone/.

⁴⁷ Carl Franzen, *How the Web Killed SOPA and PIPA*, TPM, Jan. 20, 2012, http://idealab.talkingpointsmemo.com/2012/01/how-the-web-killed-sopa-and-pipa.php.

⁴⁸ H.R. 3782 – OPEN Act, *available at* http://beta.congress.gov/bill/112th-congress/house-bill/3782/cosponsors.

⁴⁹ Michael Cieply & Edward Wyatt, *Dodd Calls for Hollywood and Silicon Valley to Meet*, N.Y. TIMES, Jan. 19, 2012, http://www.nytimes.com/2012/01/20/technology/dodd-calls-for-hollywood-and-silicon-valley-to-meet.html.

⁵⁰ Press Release by MPAA Chairman and CEO Chris Dodd on the So-Called "Blackout Day" Protesting Anti-Piracy Legislation, Jan. 17, 2012, http://mpaa.org/resources/c4c3712a-7b9f-4be8-bd70-25527d5dfad8.pdf.

⁵¹ Brendan Sasso, *Chamber Study Finds Intellectual Property Industries Produce $5 Trillion*, THE HILL, May 23, 2012, http://thehill.com/blogs/hillicon-valley/technology/229147-chamber-study-finds-intellectual-property-industries-produce-5-trillion.

Chapter 5: NO to ACTA

¹ *Wikipedia and Google Protest US Net Bills*, SYDNEY MORNING HERALD, Jan. 18, 2012, http://www.smh.com.au/technology/technology-news/wikipedia-and-google-protest-us-net-bills-20120118-1q6ac.html; *Uncle Sam Found Wanting*, THE HERALD, Jan. 19, 2012, http://www.herald.co.zw/uncle-sam-found-wanting/.

² Shi Jianfeng, *Wikipedia Shut Down 24 Hours to Protest "Anti-Piracy Laws,"* SOHU, Jan. 18, 2012, http://roll.sohu.com/20120118/n332502331.shtml; Ruan YiFeng, About Me, http://www.ruanyifeng.com/about.html.

³ Ruan Yifeng, *Why SOPA Is a Bad Law*, RuanYifeng.com, Jan. 17, 2012, http://www.ruanyifeng.com/blog/2012/01/why_sopa_is_evil.html.

⁴ Jack Goldsmith & Lawrence Lessig, *Anti-Counterfeiting Agreement Raises Constitutional Concerns*, WASH. POST, March 26, 2010, http://www.washingtonpost.com/wp-dyn/content/article/2010/03/25/AR2010032502403.html.

⁵ Letter from Harold Koh, Legal Adviser to the State Department, to Senator Wyden, March 6, 2012, *available at* http://infojustice.org/wp-content/uploads/2012/03/84365507-State-Department-Response-to-Wyden-on-ACTA.pdf.

⁶ Letter from Senator Wyden to Harold Koh, Legal Adviser, July 25, 2012, *available at* http://infojustice.org/wp-content/uploads/2012/07/wyden-07252012.pdf; Letter from Law Professors to Senate Committee on Finance, May 16, 2012, *available at* http://infojustice.org/wp-content/uploads/2012/05/Law-Professor-Letter-to-Senate-Finance-Committee-May-16-20122.pdf; Jack Goldsmith,

The Doubtful Constitutionality of ACTA as an Ex Ante Congressional-Executive Agreement, May 21, 2012, http://www.lawfareblog.com/2012/05/the-doubtful-constitutionality-of-acta-as-an-ex-ante-congressional-executive-agreement/.

⁷ Conseil constitutionnel [CC] [Constitutional Court], No. 2009-580DC, June 10, 2009, *relative à la loi favorisant la diffusion et la protection de la création sur internet*, June 13, 2009, JOURNAL OFFICIEL DE LA RÉPUBLIQUE FRANÇAISE [J.O.], at 9675.

⁸ ACTA art. 27(1), available at http://www.mofa.go.jp/policy/economy/i_property/pdfs/acta1105_en.pdf.

⁹ *Protest Przeciwko SOPA i PIPA*, NEWSFIX, Jan. 18, 2012, http://www.newsfix.pl/index.php/2012/01/18/protest-przeciwko-sopa-i-pipa/.

¹⁰ Rysiek, *Hacking for Change: Anti-ACTA in Poland – Seen from the Inside*, EDGERYDERS, March 28, 2012, http://edgeryders.wikispiral.org/welcome-group/mission_case/anti-acta-poland-seen-inside.

¹¹ POLAND 2030 REPORT, http://zds.kprm.gov.pl/en/poland-2030-report.

¹² Igor Ostrowsky, TWITTER, Jan. 19, 2012, https://twitter.com/IgorOstrowski/status/159969972175642624.

¹³ Piotr VaGla Waglowski, *ACTA: Sukces Polskiej Prezydencji, Polska Podpisze Umowę 26 Stycznia w Tokio*, http://prawo.vagla.pl/node/9631.

¹⁴ *About ACTA at Polish PM Chancellery*, RYSIOBRAG, Jan. 19, 2012, http://rys.io/en/59.

¹⁵ Czy Polsce Grozi Cenzura Internetu w Imię Ochrony Praw Autorskich? Z Naszych Najświeższych Informacji Wynika, że tak!, PAHOPTIKON FOUNDATION, Jan. 19, 2012, http://panoptykon.org/wiadomosc/czy-polsce-grozi-cenzura-internetu-w-imie-ochrony-praw-autorskich-z-naszych-najswiezszych-.

¹⁶ Tomasz Grynkiewicz, *Internet AD ACTA?*, GAZETA WYBORCZA, Jan. 20, 2012, at 1.

¹⁷ Jared T. Miller, *The Dotcom Mansion*, TIME NEWSFEED, Jan. 24, 2012, http://newsfeed.time.com/2012/01/24/photos-the-larger-than-life-lifestyle-of-megauploads-kim-dotcom/slide/the-dotcom-mansion/.

¹⁸ Charles Graeber, *Inside the Mansion—and the Mind—of Kim Dotcom, the Most Wanted Man on the Net*, WIRED, Oct. 18, 2012, http://www.wired.com/threatlevel/2012/10/ff-kim-dotcom/.

¹⁹ *Mr. Kim Dotcom, Kim Dotcom Megaupload Song HD*, YouTUBE, Dec. 17, 2011, http://youtu.be/o0Wvn-9BXVc.

²⁰ *New Zealand Police Search and Seizure of Megaupload Property Declared Illegal*, INFOSECURITY MAGAZINE, June 28, 2012, http://www.infosecurity-magazine.com/view/26659/new-zealand-police-search-and-seizure-of-megaupload-property-declared-illegal.

²¹ Greg Sandoval, *New Zealand PM Apologizes to Kim Dotcom; Case Unraveling*, CNET, Sept. 27, 2012, http://news.cnet.com/8301-1023_3-57521208-93/new-zealand-pm-apologizes-to-kim-dotcom-case-unraveling/.

²² Sari Horwitz & Cecilia Kang, *Federal Indictment Claims Popular Web site Megaupload.com Shared Pirated Material*, WASH. POST, Jan. 19, 2012, http://articles.washingtonpost.com/2012-01-19/business/35440354_1_web-sites-hackers-largest-criminal-copyright-ca.

[23] Rysiek, *supra* note 178 (emphasis omitted).

[24] *Ogloszenie Stanu Wojennego – 13 Gru 1981*, YOUTUBE, Jan. 21, 2012, http://youtu.be/dKhITm9-5TU; JARUZELKSI, PRIME MINISTER OF POLAND: SELECTED SPEECHES 28-34 (Robert Maxwell ed. 1985)...

[25] *Panie Premiere, Przejmujemy Kontrole*, YOUTUBE, Jan. 21, 2012, http://youtu.be/QKAH3Xj1bQc.

[26] Marcin Sobczyk, *Hackers Hit Polish Government Websites*, WALL ST. J. EUROPE, Jan. 23, 2012, http://blogs.wsj.com/emergingeurope/2012/01/23/hackers-hit-polish-government-websites/.

[27] Anonymous, TWITTER, Jan. 22, 2012, https://twitter.com/AnonymousWiki/statuses/160980628739862528.

[28] Anonymous, TWITTER, Jan. 22, 2012, https://twitter.com/AnonymousWiki/status/161159648395804672.

[29] *PM Tusk Stands Firm on ACTA Despite Internet Attacks*, THE NEWS POLAND, Jan. 24, 2012, http://www.thenews.pl/1/10/Artykul/84150,PM-Tusk-stands-firm-on-ACTA-despite-internet-attacks.

[30] *Attacks on Polish Sites Must Stop NOW*, Jan. 24, 2012, http://pastebin.com/1mDAceCF.

[31] *Oswiadczenie Organizacji Pozarzadowych Dotyczace Stanowiska Poliskiego Rzadu Wobe ACTA*, Jan. 22, 2012, http://nowoczesnapolska.org.pl/wp-content/uploads/2012/01/acta_oswiadczenie-organizacji_23-01-2012_l.pdf.

[32] *Nie dla ACTA w Polsce*, FACEBOOK, https://www.facebook.com/nieACTA.

[33] Wiktor Szpunar, *Powiedzieli "NIE" dla ACTA w Polsce - Rozmowa z Organizatorami Akcji*, PC WORLD, Feb. 17, 2012, http://www.pcworld.pl/news/380342/Powiedzieli.NIE.dla.ACTA.w.Polsce.rozmowa.z.organizatorami.akcji.html.

[34] *Nie dla ACTA SOPA PIPA Krakow*, FACEBOOK, https://www.facebook.com/NieDlaActaKrakow?ref=stream.

[35] *Nie dla ACTA - Kraków (wydarzenie dynamiczne)*, FACEBOOK, https://www.facebook.com/events/215317315225357/.

[36] *Protest Przeciwko ACTA - Warszawa 24.01.2012*, YOUTUBE, Jan. 24, 2012, http://youtu.be/un71wZY5Rno?t=1m55s.

[37] *Protest Przeciwko Podpisaniu ACTA*, LOVE KRAKOW, http://lovekrakow.pl/galerie/zdjecie/id/1176.

Chapter 6: Hello, Democracy

[1] Ministry of Foreign Affairs of Japan, *Signing Ceremony of the EU for the Anti-Counterfeiting Trade Agreement*, Jan. 26, 2012, http://www.mofa.go.jp/policy/economy/i_property/acta1201.html.

[2] *Nie dla ACTA*, FACEBOOK, https://www.facebook.com/events/301294013254264/ (entry of Agnieszka Broszkiewicz, January 26, 2012, 1:59 a.m.).

[3] David Meyer, *MEP Quits ACTA 'Charade" in Protest at EU Signing*, ZDNET, Jan. 26, 2012, http://www.zdnet.com/mep-quits-acta-charade-in-protest-at-eu-signing-4010025297/.

[4] *"Internauci mają rację" - Tusk zawiesza ratyfikację ACTA*, WIADOMOSCI, Feb. 3, 2012, http://wiadomosci.wp.pl/title,Internauci-maja-racje-Tusk-zawiesza-

ratyfikacje-ACTA,wid,14224470,wiadomosc.html?ticaid=1fbb8.

[5] Quinn Norton, *How the European Internet Rose Up Against ACTA*, WIRED, Feb. 21, 2012, http://www.wired.com/threatlevel/2012/02/europe-acta/.

[6] *Debata wolność i prawa w Internecie ACTA Donald Tusk 2012.02.06 - cała Debata!*, YouTube, Feb. 7, 2012, http://youtu.be/cnT4ZVhWa-o.

[7] David Meyer, *Tusk Gores ACTA*, ZDNET, Feb. 18, 2012, http://www.zdnet.com/polands-tusk-gores-acta-4010025437/.

[8] ELECTRONIC ARTS, BATTLEFIELD3, http://www.battlefield.com/battlefield3/1/destruction.

[9] *Der Teufel im Vertragsdetail*, GAMESTAR, Oct. 25, 2011, http://www.gamestar.de/spiele/battlefield-3/artikel/analyse_zur_eula_von_ea_origin,45612,2561554.html.

[10] Von Konrad Lischka, *Electronic Arts: Spiele-Gigant will Kunden ausspionieren*, SPIEGEL ONLINE, Oct. 28, 2011, http://www.spiegel.de/netzwelt/netzpolitik/electronic-arts-spiele-gigant-will-kunden-ausspionieren-a-794600.html.

[11] Sebastian Radtke, *ACTA and SOPA*, THE ORIGIN, Dec. 19, 2011, http://www.theorigin.de/old/wordpress/?p=2563.

[12] Pirate Party UK, *What's in a Name?*, May 4, 2010, http://www.pirateparty.org.uk/blog/2010/may/4/whats-name/.

[13] TEDxTalks, *TEDxObserver - Rick Falkvinge - The Pirate Party - the Politics of Protest*, YouTube, May 21, 2012, http://youtu.be/zsI3-IEWgFg.

[14] Pirate Party, *Manifesto of the Pirate Party of Germany: English Version*, http://wiki.piratenpartei.de/Parteiprogramm/en.

[15] Thumay, TWITTER, Jan. 29, 2012, https://twitter.com/hope_74/status/163622293845708801.

[16] *See* STOPP ACTA, http://www.stopp-acta.info.

[17] Markus Beckedahl, *How to Build an Anti-ACTA Campaign*, June 20, 2012, https://digitalegesellschaft.de/2012/06/how-to-build-an-anti-acta-campaign/.

[18] EU Commission, *10 Myths About ACTA*, http://trade.ec.europa.eu/doclib/docs/2012/january/tradoc_148964.pdf.

[19] *ACTA Demo in Kassel 11.02.2012*, YouTube, Feb. 12, 2012, http://youtu.be/mFUmZKb9Zzs?t=2m50s.

[20] *Anti-ACTA Protests Spread Across Europe*, ALJAZEERA, Feb. 11, 2012, http://stream.aljazeera.com/story/anti-acta-protests-spread-across-europe-0022037.

[21] *RObotzi.S02.Ep.Special.ACTA*, CREATIVEMONKEYZ, http://creativemonkeyz.com/roboti/robotzi-s02-ep-special-acta/.

[22] Laura Muresan, *Anti A.C.T.A. Protest in Cluj-Napoca, the 11 of February 2012*, iREPORT CNN, Feb. 11, 2012, http://ireport.cnn.com/docs/DOC-746395

[23] *Protest against ACTA - 11.02.2012, Sofia, Bulgaria*, YouTube, Feb. 11, 2012, http://youtu.be/6Y59XxJoStA

[24] Luis Miranda, *Europeans Protest Against ACTA Censorship*, THE REAL AGENDA, Feb. 11, 2012, http://real-agenda.com/2012/02/11/europeans-protest-against-acta-censorship/.

[25] Jack Phillips, *ACTA Protests Spring Up Across Europe*, EPOCH TIMES, Feb. 13, 2012, http://www.theepochtimes.com/n2/world/acta-protests-spring-up-across-europe-190046.html.

[26] *ACTA: A Message to Poland from Mainz (Germany)*, YouTube, Feb. 11, 2012, http://youtu.be/OJ6qvCgaDGE.

[27] Bronislaw Komorowski, Twitter, Feb. 10, 2012, https://twitter.com/PlaidKomorowski/status/168146767597146112.

[28] *What Makes ACTA So Controversial (and Why MEPs Should Care)*, https://s3.amazonaws.com/access.3cdn.net/7e0f407b02b968cbb6_vrm6iyv2t.pdf.

[29] Access Now, *Just Say 'No' to ACTA*, https://www.accessnow.org/page/s/just-say-no-to-acta.

[30] Avaaz, *ACTA: The New Threat to the Net*, https://secure.avaaz.org/en/eu_save_the_internet/.

[31] Ben Rooney, *Europe's Most Wired Politician*, Wall St. J. Tech Europe, June 17, 2011, http://blogs.wsj.com/tech-europe/2011/06/17/marietje-schaake-europes-most-wired-politician/.

[32] *ACTA stakeholder HEARING*, YouTube, April 20, 2012, http://youtu.be/_2Y-9fPNY_V0.

.

8491618R00101

Made in the USA
San Bernardino, CA
10 February 2014